GARDEN

LUNACY

A GROWING CONCERN

GARDEN LUNACY

A GROWING CONCERN

BY

ART WOLK

AAB Book Publishing LLC
Voorhees, New Jersey
Books that enrich, entertain, and enlighten

AAB

Published by AAB Book Publishing LLC, P.O. Box 749 Voorhees, NJ 08043.
First Edition.

Visit our website at www.gardenlunacy.com.

First printed January 2005

Cataloging-in-Publication Data
Wolk, Art
    Garden Lunacy: a growing concern /
    Art Wolk.—1st ed.
        p. cm.
    Includes bibliographic references and footnotes.
    ISBN 0-9729730-3-6
1. Gardening—Humor. 2. Gardeners—Anecdotes
3. Gardening—Anecdotes 4. Flowers shows—Humor
5. Flower Shows—Anecdotes. I. Title.
SB455.W6   c2005
635.0207—dc22
                    Library of Congress Control Number: 2003093188
                    OCLC number: 55200288

AAB Book Publishing LLC, P.O. Box 749, Voorhees, NJ 08043
www.aabbookpublishing.com

10 9 8 7 6 5 4 3 2 1

Prices in text valid to December 2005

Jacket illustration and design by Wendell Minor
Editor Pete Johnson, copy editor Barbara J. Crawford
Interior illustration by Laurie Baxendell, Baxendell Graphics
Interior Design by Laurie Baxendell and Art Wolk
Jacket photo by Krassan and Kovnat Photo, Marlton, NJ

This book was printed on recycled paper

How to contact the author:

Art Wolk is available for speeches and can be contacted at the address below. Readers of this book are also encouraged to contact the author with comments and ideas for future editions.

Art Wolk, AAB Book Publishing LLC
P.O. Box 749
Voorhees, NJ 08043
Phone: (856)-751-8286
GardenLunacy@aol.com
Web site: www.gardenlunacy.com

To Arlene, Beth, and Mom

Contents

6: GARDENERS AND NON-GARDENERS

7: ABERRANT BEHAVIOR IN GARDENERS

8: FLOWER SHOWS — PART TWO

9: GARDEN TELEVISION AND MAGAZINES

10: DID YOU EVER THINK ABOUT ...?

Acknowledgements

This book would not have been possible without the unflagging support given to me by my wife, Arlene, and daughter, Beth. They are non-gardeners who read every word of this book and gave me invaluable suggestions.

I would also like to thank my cover illustrator, Wendell Minor, for his creativity and enthusiasm for this project. In addition, I am grateful to interior illustrator and designer Lorie Baxendell, whose talent and sense of humor are conveyed in every drawing.

I also wish to thank my editors, Pete Johnson and Barbara Crawford, whose help was invaluable. Furthermore, I'm indebted to Lisa Derfler and Lorrie Baggett-Heuser, whose cataloging expertise made it possible for readers to find this book.

I was blessed to have teachers and other adults that broadened my world and help me reach my potential. I especially want to thank Marilyn Popp, my fourth grade teacher, who was the first person to start me down the path toward becoming a gardener. Jean Byrne, my first magazine editor, was also of great importance. She endured my unending questions and saw a spark of writing talent that could be nurtured and developed.

In addition, I owe so much to the Pennsylvania Horticultural Society (PHS). For me and many other gardeners of the world, it is the premiere horticultural organization. In addition, the PHS wouldn't have become a world-class gardening institution without the guidance of two wonderful visionaries: Ernesta Ballard and Jane Pepper. Ernesta congratulated me when I won my first blue ribbon, and Jane was a very positive influence when I stretched my horticultural wings wider. When I heard how much she enjoyed a magazine article I had written, I felt like royalty.

Rita Hojnowski has also been invaluable, for both her friendship and devotion to my local garden club's newsletter. Simply by saying, "Would you like to write a president's article each month?" I started writing more about gardeners than gardening.

Several relatives have been my horticultural cheerleaders, including my in-laws, Sylvia and Louis Budman, and my Aunt Shirley,

Uncle Jerry and Aunt Elaine. In addition, my Aunt Gert and Cousin Gil have been the best fans a writer could have: they've maintained a scrapbook of my gardening accomplishments for over a decade.

My indefatigable friends who made possible my success at the Philadelphia Flower Show include Todd Sokol, Joan Hemphill, Bill and Mary Harkell, Claudia Sumler, Ellie Lloyd, Brian and Ruth Nielsen, Joan Smith, Pete Parker, Meg and Rich Goode, Vicki Berberian, Marie Lamancusa, Claudia Sumler, Judy Gates, Monica Dubel, and Barbara Ogle.

I am also indebted to Liz Ball, Ellen Spector-Platt, and Betty Mackey who helped guide me through the various stages of my career as a garden writer. Liz unknowingly gave me the greatest compliment I've ever received from a fellow garden writer: She asked permission to photocopy a humorous article I had written for a national magazine. It made me realize that gardeners have a hunger for published garden humor, but find almost none.

Introduction

What is at the other end of a shovel?

You've already used the metal pointy end to plant hundreds or thousands of shrubs, trees, vegetables, and flowering plants. You already own dozens, if not hundreds, of books that either show you the plants on which to use the pointy end, how and when to use the pointy end, pictures of gardens that were made with the pointy end, or which gardens to visit that were created with the pointy end.

But shovels also have another end — a wooden end. Attached to that end are gardeners, but we have very few books about them. Who are they? What are their feelings? Their ups and downs? Their strengths and weaknesses? And why do they see and think about the world so differently from non-gardeners?

Why do they grip the shovel's wooden end to turn under and kill grass to create front yard flowerbeds, when their neighbors think of grass as the ultimate suburban art form? Why do gardeners keep every fallen leaf for mulch or compost, while their non-gardening neighbors throw them away? Why do gardeners visit properties, only to remember the botanical residents outside the houses, but none of the décor added by the human residents inside?

In fact, gardeners and non-gardeners exist on the same planet but in separate worlds, possessing different values, vocabularies, and ideas of acceptable behavior.

Non-gardeners have the sense to get rid of a tree that poses a danger to their home, while gardeners see such a step as sacrilegious. Indeed, while plants run the gamut from the miniscule to the gargantuan, gardeners find it hard to eliminate a single one. To the contrary, ardent gardeners seem to want one of everything, and will stop at nothing to own coveted plants — even if it means risking humiliation if they're caught stealing a cutting.

Gardeners process information in a way that is completely foreign to non-gardeners. A gardener can watch a movie and become enthralled, until something appears botanically askew — like North American wildflowers in a movie supposedly taking place in Asia. As a result, the film is never again held in high regard by the gardener. But non-gardeners may consider the same movie to be one of the best they've ever seen, and haven't the faintest idea why the gardener is so perturbed.

Non-gardeners welcome deer, groundhogs, and rabbits to their yards, but their polar opposites plan military-like campaigns against them. Gardeners experience no greater pleasure than expelling a tormenting plant-eater from their garden, while non-gardeners are appalled by a gardener's ill will toward these seemingly innocuous creatures.

Many gardeners are flower show exhibitors who go through hell for the chance to win blue ribbons and silver cups. A behind-the-scenes glimpse at these shows reveals the extreme devotion and occasional overheated competitiveness of the entrants. More than anything else on earth, these shows are great class levelers, with poor and middle-class people exhibiting plants alongside multi-millionaires. And regardless of social class, all exhibitors experience the same emotions after judging is completed, from the heights of euphoria to the feeling that they need to call a crisis-intervention hotline. Winning awards at these shows can be likened to an addiction to heroin, for it is horticultural heroines and heroes that all exhibitors want to become — year, after year, after year.

Gardeners can't understand why their non-gardening relatives, neighbors, and friends make such a fuss when dragged to these winter shows. Ultimately, non-gardeners swear they'd rather spend a lifetime in the Sahara than another ten minutes accompanying a gardener to a flower show.

Gardeners might hate having relatives visit their homes, but are quite willing to let gardeners who are total strangers visit their backyards. So it comes as no surprise that gardeners find one another. Like bees in a hive, they congregate in the world's garden clubs. These groups run the gamut: from those specializing in one type of plant, to those that are social clubs masquerading as garden clubs, to those like the Pennsylvania Horticultural Society that come close to being all things to all gardeners.

If you're a non-gardener who's curious enough to read this book, I don't expect you to convert, but you'll laugh at the descriptions of behaviors common to all gardeners. If you can gain one bit of understanding, it's this: Gardeners are addicted to the hardest of all hobbies to master. Unachievable perfection is sought, but never attained. We want our handiwork to be appreciated, admired, and envied, and will do anything it takes to achieve those ends, whether our gardens are as small as a few potted plants or as expansive as estates.

To my fellow gardeners: My intention is never to belittle, but to give you a rollicking laugh. As you'll discover, I probably have more horticultural foibles and addictions than any gardener you've ever met. If you identify with any of my eccentricities, I hope you'll be able to laugh along with me. There's enough sadness and grief in the world. So take this opportunity to inject a little joy and laughter into your life, whether you're a novice or a lifelong holder of the wooden end of the shovel.

" Aren't you afraid of the GREENHOUSE effect?"

A Digger's Dictionary

Not long ago, someone introduced me to a new member of my local garden club as an "expert gardener." And, while I appreciated the compliment, I wasn't sure the new member understood the terminology. She stood there and didn't know whether to shake my hand, kneel, or laugh in my face.

I was conscious of the new member's dilemma, and realized that the problem stemmed from the jargon thrown around at our meetings. So, in an effort to reduce the number of new members who drop out of their local garden clubs because they don't speak "Gardenese," I've provided a digger's dictionary. It may help horticultural organizations retain members. But more importantly, it'll help me get the exact amount of, meaning lack of, respect I deserve.

bamboo: A plant bought as an infant to create a small vertical background in the garden. Instead, gardeners find that they've installed a behemoth that grows thirty feet tall, and is so invasive that it takes them twenty minutes to find the front door after parking in their driveways.

borer: A garden club member who induces sleep by telling the same story about his four-pound tomatoes at every meeting.

compost pile: A heap containing soil, manure, and garden plants that were supposed to yield flowers and vegetables, but died while under the gardener's care.

d-rt: The offensive four-letter word used by non-gardeners instead of "soil." They do this because they think soil is something to be avoided, since it makes them d-rty.

dungarees: Pants that gardeners wear while working in their backyards. Retailers managed to triple their price simply by renaming them "jeans."

fence: A barrier that gardeners erect to keep out deer, groundhogs, and ball-retrieving kids with size twelve sneakers. In reality, it succeeds in none of these endeavors, but gardeners delude themselves into believing otherwise.

flower show: A place where blue-ribbon winners go to smile, gloat, and shake the hands of non-winners. Upon arriving home, these same non-winners stick pins in voodoo dolls that look exactly like the winners.

garden: An equal opportunity employer of the earth's most eccentric people, who together produce enough flowers and vegetables to feed all of the world's insects, groundhogs, raccoons, and deer.

garden center: A store where gardeners go to spend $5 for things they don't need, but end up spending $105 for things they don't need.

garden club: A convivial place for gardeners to get together to sensationalize their successes while soft-pedaling their failures.

gardeners: People who try to keep plants alive in and around their homes. They're divided into the following categories based on their level of expertise:
- **novice gardener**: Someone who hasn't gardened long enough to kill one hundred plants.
- **experienced gardener**: Someone who's gardened long enough to kill one thousand plants.
- **expert gardener**: Someone who's qualified to tell others how to kill ten thousand plants.
- **author of this book**: Someone who makes money writing and lecturing about how he killed one hundred thousand plants in fewer than twenty-five years.

greenhouse: The gardener's heaven-on-earth. It raises the cost of growing a seedling from $5 to $500, which is why it takes sixty years for gardeners to convince their spouses that they need one. Alas, this is fifty-five years longer than most gardener/non-gardener marriages last.

greenhouse effect: Once gardeners are lucky enough to own a greenhouse, they're unlucky enough to be smitten with this personality disorder. The symptoms include

- believing that their greenhouse is too small, even if it's larger than their house;
- acquiring three times more plants than the greenhouse will hold; and
- reaching the point where the gardener doesn't own the greenhouse, but the greenhouse owns the gardener.

green supremacists: People who think that their front lawns should stay green from April to November, regardless of drought conditions. They're ready to use any chemical to maintain their lawn, and can usually be found caring for and mowing it at 6:30AM every Saturday morning. They compare themselves with their neighbors based on the greenness and lack of diversity of their lawn. No temperate zone green supremacist can accept the idea that lawn grasses naturally go dormant and turn brown in hot weather.

groundhogs: The original outdoor vacuum cleaners. They can suck up anything not cemented to the home's foundation, and have been known to induce apoplexy and asphyxia in gardeners.

hortiholics: Humans who attach so much importance to gardening, that it influences every facet of their lives. The number of plants acquired by hortiholics increases as quickly as their funds decrease. In its worst stages, plants are hidden from family members. All non-gardeners view hortiholics with the same respect given to the village idiot in Renaissance Europe.

hybrid tea rose: A plant hybridized by botanists to be drought intolerant and susceptible to attack by every fungus and insect pest on the planet.

non-gardeners: See Chapter 6 — all of it. Neither a sentence, nor a paragraph, nor an entire page were enough to describe this oddball group of humans.

plant mafia: People who purchase new, extravagant plant hybrids. They are either wealthy gardeners or those willing to take out a second mortgage on their homes to acquire these plants. The hybridizers surrender their creations because they're given "an offer they can't refuse."

plantslaughter (as in *plant slaughter*, not *plants laughter*): The botanical version of manslaughter, namely, the involuntary killing of plants. Fortunately, this hasn't become a criminal offense. If it ever does, gardeners would fill the jails and become extremely involuntary indoor horticulturists.

rabbits: Garden marauders with extraordinary mental powers. They send subliminal messages to gardeners, making us believe that the way to keep them out of our gardens is to plant marigolds, which are, of course, their most preferred food.

rake: A garden tool constructed to hit gardeners squarely between the eyes when stored on the ground in the usual tines-up position.

rototiller: A machine used by gardeners to avoid the backbreaking work of turning under the soil. In reality, this machine is so heavy and bounces around so much that it causes displaced vertebrae in gardeners otherwise hearty enough to win Olympic gold medals for weight lifting.

seasons: Three-month segments marked by obsessive thoughts and compulsive behaviors among all gardeners. More specifically:
- **spring**: The season when gardeners rush the growing season by planting annuals when the temperature first hits 65°F, even though it's four weeks before the last frost.
- **summer**: The season when gardeners spend money on water, fertilizer, tomato cages, bamboo stakes, and topsoil; and time on weeding, spreading mulch, killing insects, chasing groundhogs, and harvesting enough vegetables to make one salad.
- **fall**: The season when gardeners come back from vacation to discover that their garden has become a humiliating, irreparable mess.

- **winter**: The season when gardeners' power bills reach astronomical levels because of the electric lights needed to keep indoor plants growing when they should be dormant.

seed catalog: An instrument of temptation so salacious that its producers have wisely decided to send it to gardeners wrapped in brown paper.

soil test: The test done by one out of every ten thousand gardeners, who are then entitled to join the ranks of millions of other gardeners confounded by the mysteries of soil.

topiary: A form of horticultural torment that forces plants to grow into unnatural shapes so that their owners can impress other gardeners unskilled in the art of plant torture.

trowel: A tool made for gardeners who move plants from the left side of the garden to the right, and back again every year. They're constructed to last at least ten years, but only last two because most gardeners use them as hammers.

zonal denial:* Behavior exhibited by gardeners who are either delusional or who think the people who work for the U.S. Department of Agriculture are delusional. Typically, they believe that semitropical plants can survive in places like North Dakota, Wisconsin, and Montana. This belief gives them the chance to completely redesign their gardens every spring, since the remains of their plants end up on compost heaps at the end of every winter.

Now that we've got most of the terminology out of the way, you can understand why I'm so eminently qualified to be the author of this book, and why I deserve a certain measure of respect for having the largest compost pile in New Jersey.

---

*See *Are You Zoned Out?*, page 219.

"I only have another 137 plant names to
jot down...isn't this just great?!"

1

COMMANDMENTS FOR REAL GARDENERS

Are You for Real?

WE'RE CONSTANTLY DELUGED WITH lists that declare which of us are "real" men or "real" women. But these lists don't make sense for gardeners, because our hobby is gender-neutral and the usual stereotypes don't apply. A trip to the home of many gardeners reveals that men are doing delicate flower arranging and women are working with heavy garden equipment. And, that's all to the good.

But that begs the question of what exactly a "real" gardener happens to be. Based on my experience, I offer the following list of traits that you'll recognize and perhaps emulate. However, I don't recommend that you adopt all of them, because if you do, your family will see to it that you and your plants are suddenly homeless.

- Real gardeners spend more money on plants than their clothes, and they look it!
- Real gardeners have a home library with one bible, one cookbook, one dictionary, one novel, one biography, and two hundred books on how to plant a bean seed.
- Real gardeners find it impossible to throw away an invitation to join their twentieth plant society.
- Real gardeners buy at least ten thousand plants in the course of a lifetime without having the least idea where they'll put any of them when they get home.
- Real gardeners don't care what anyone thinks of them when they steal their neighbors' bags of grass clippings for mulch.
- Real gardeners let their world come to a grinding halt whenever a total stranger asks to see their garden.

- Real gardeners never get completely clean.
- Real gardeners don't think there's anything cute and fuzzy about rabbits, groundhogs, raccoons, or deer.
- Real gardeners think that anyone who buys tomatoes from a supermarket in the summer should be committed.
- Real gardeners break the land speed record to get their fresh-picked corn into boiling water.
- Real gardeners have soil under their nails from every garden they've ever planted.
- Real gardeners have one hammer, one saw, one screwdriver, and seventeen different shovels.
- Real gardeners forever hope that they haven't won their last blue ribbon.
- Real gardeners are surrounded by neighbors who think they're crazy. (But we know non-gardeners are really the crazy ones!)
- Real gardeners become psychotic before every flower show in which they compete, driving themselves and everyone around them to the brink of insanity. Then they're ready to endure the same agonies again if they win just one blue ribbon.
- Real gardeners know a garden is never perfect because there are always at least thirty more things to get done.
- Real gardeners think that "Deer Crossing" signs are notices of opportunity, not hazard.
- Real gardeners tour public and private gardens with notebooks, so they can drive their families loony while taking half a day to write down the name of every intriguing plant they see.
- Real gardeners don't look up to presidents, prime ministers, or sports heroes. The object of their adulation is the author of the most expensive garden book at their local bookstore.
- Real gardeners are so cheap that they save seeds for at least twenty years, but willingly spend a fortune over the course of a lifetime for garden gadgets that break after ten minutes of use.
- Real gardeners think all of God's creatures deserve a place in the universe, except, of course, for plant-eaters living in the universe of a gardener's backyard.
- Real gardeners, during their lifetime, kill five thousand plants that would have survived perfectly well without any "assistance."

- Real gardeners know their gardens change size during the course of a year. When they order seeds and plants in the winter, their gardens are the size of a football field. At planting time in the spring, their gardens are the size of a postage stamp. When it's 100°F outside in August, their gardens are the size of three football fields. And in the fall, when it's time to clean up, their gardens don't exist at all!
- Real gardeners know they're going to live forever. Why else would a ninety-year-old gardener plant two oak tree seedlings, then look through a catalog for a hammock?

The Gardener's Ten Commandments

Virtually all garden writers dispense commandments, telling you how to design your garden, which plants you should grow, and how you should grow them. Worse yet, every year there seems to be a different set of dictums for the same gardening activities. It forces gardeners to decide which horticultural "deity" to follow — assuming they can religiously follow even one set of commandments.

After thirty years, I've hit on some sure-fire commandments that all gardeners can follow. And the only house of worship needed to remember them is right in their backyards.

1. Thou shalt covet thy neighbor's plants.

    Do I really have to explain this one? Are there any gardeners who haven't either used pretidigitation to steal cuttings or at least given it serious thought?

2. Thou shalt either be eccentric or find eccentrics charming.

    Am I the only one who's noticed that garden clubs attract people that are more than a bit off-center?

3. Thou shalt be able to read a road map.

    Since the best public garden, plant, fertilizer, or potting mix is always just out of reach, you have to be able to find it on a map. In my home state of New Jersey, it's especially necessary to be able to read a U.S. Geological Survey Map, since the name of a road can change five times in less than five miles.

4. Thou shalt forsake thy fingernails.

    Have you ever seen an avid gardener with pristine nails? There's nothing that makes me take to gardeners faster than the sight of soil under their nails. But I prefer to see it when they're gardening, not when they're serving me lunch.

5. Thou shalt obsess about the weather.

   Why don't they quit the charade already and call the Weather Channel the Gardeners' Channel? Whether richer or poorer, in sickness or in health, gardeners always have one ear cocked for the weather. I think that if I'm on my deathbed and I hear about frost warnings, my last words to my wife will be, "Please close the cold frames, dear."*

6. Thou shalt keep an open mind.

   This is absolutely essential, because no matter how unequivocal the rules are about growing a plant, some better way will be espoused next year.

7. Thy favorite ribbon shalt be of nylon and thy chosen color for said nylon shalt be blue.

   Non-gardeners don't understand this, but those eight square inches of blue material have caused more obsessive-compulsive behavior in gardeners than their health, jobs, or families. Tell me if I'm wrong, but I don't think there's been a single flower show exhibitor who was serious when saying, "I've won enough blue ribbons, I think I'll let someone else have a chance."

8. Thou shalt order twenty times more seeds than thou needest.

   No truer words were ever spoken than when Henry Wadsworth Longfellow said, "After the Garden Of Eden, man's great temptation occurred when he first received his seed catalog."†
   If there's ever a school for con men, the first training manual will be a seed catalog. The colors, pictures, and descriptions would tempt any skinflint gardener to buy twenty packets for a garden of only ten square feet.

---

*A cold frame is a small garden structure, partially buried in the ground, with windows that slant toward the sun. Cold frames extend the growing season for gardeners, allowing them to grow plants inside the frames later in the fall and earlier in the spring.

†*Gardens of the World with Audrey Hepburn*, vol. 5, Country Gardens, VHS, directed by Bruce Franchini (Pasadena, CA; Perennial Productions, 1993).

9. Thou shalt not give a damn about soil spilt in your car or trunk.
    Since you never know when you might discover a perfect plant for sale by a home gardener, you have to be ready to transport it home — even if you've just had your car washed.

10. Thou shalt appreciate each day and the joys it reveals.
    In my opinion, gardeners have eternal faith in the future. We're always doing something today that will lead to the glories of tomorrow. More importantly, it's watching the process along the way that avid gardeners love most. Watching bean seedlings emerge from the soil is just as joyous as the harvest. Enjoy every minute!

The Real Zeal of Organic Gardeners

It seems so simple: Return to nature only what nature has given you, meaning leaves, manure, soil, and their magical amalgam — compost.

Before we learned how to break down nature into its chemical components, this was how humanity grew plants. So when the chemicals we created led to contaminated groundwater, superfund sites, and nuclear meltdowns, many of us adopted this simple creed, becoming organic gardeners by default.

Over the decades it's become obvious that real organic gardeners, the truly zealous ones, also share other traits. And while the rest of the world may consider organic gardeners peculiar, I tend to look at them as the only true gardeners in a world gone mad.

Here are just a few of the traits that set them apart:

♈ Real organic gardeners are the only people who roll down their windows when they drive past a cow pasture.

♈ Real organic gardeners give *Organic Gardening* magazines to religious missionaries who come to their doors.

♈ Real organic gardeners dig in their backyards wearing clothes that are soil-colored even after they're washed.

♈ Real organic gardeners taught Ebenezer Scrooge the meaning of the word "frugal."

♈ Real organic gardeners use elitist garden catalogs for mulch, and nothing else.

♈ Real organic gardeners think the only soil test that matters is one that measures the number of earthworms in each shovelful of their garden's loam.

♈ Real organic gardeners think the phrase "chemical fertilizer" is an oxymoron.

♈ Real organic gardeners may take trips to Jerusalem, but they make pilgrimages to the Rodale Institute.*

♈ Real organic gardeners think that flowers and leaves are interesting when they're alive, but absolutely gorgeous after being composted.

♈ Real organic gardeners don't bring in houseplants for the winter; they bring in worm boxes.

♈ Real organic gardeners keep three sacred books on the mantelpiece: the family bible, the family album, and the family copy of *Rodale's Encyclopedia of Organic Gardening*.

♈ Real organic gardeners know that cows are the world's only true alchemists, for only they can insert grass at one end and produce gold at the other.

---

*The Rodale Institute is in Maxatawny, Pennsylvania, where organic farming research is conducted.

2

AT WAR
WITH CRITTERS

Attack of the Killer Wren

IS THERE A SINGLE ONE OF YOU WHO hasn't had to do a bit of public speaking? I don't care how many times you've done it or the number of people in your audience, whether it's twelve or twelve hundred, your stomach is going to spin and leap around like Baryshnikov soaring to Tchaikovsky. I'll agree that if you do it enough, your stomach doesn't leap quite so high or spin nearly so fast, but it can still be relied upon to do its gyrations.

Given this physical response, I'm always amazed that my audience thinks I'm a relaxed, glib, master of public speaking. The truth is that before every lecture, my head feels disconnected from my neck and my stomach churns out enough acid to polish Queen Elizabeth's silver collection.

So, to keep my head attached and my stomach intact, I've devised a kind of ritual before every program. I go over the entire lecture three times the night before and once again the morning of the program. Then I use a list to make certain that I pack all the items I'll need, like a map, throat lozenges, slides, projector, extension cord, and projection screen.

Once I get to the garden club, set up, and begin speaking, I finally start to calm down. What helps is that everyone in the audience -everyone- is on your side. They want to be entertained, informed, and have a good time. Once I realized that audiences were on my side, lecturing became fun.

As you can tell, it's getting ready for a program that makes me as nervous as a condemned man listening to his scaffold being built. There's also something preternatural at work in my brain. Sometimes

I can go through my entire checklist, get the car packed, start the motor, and just as I'm ready to leave, I get a sick feeling that I've forgotten something. So I look in the back of the car and find that I've neglected to pack something important — like the projector, the map, or lecture notes. Somehow my brain knows that something is missing, and whenever my brain sends me that signal, it's right.

One morning, I had to give a lecture in Doylestown, Pennsylvania, and had done such a good job of preparing, that I had enough time to get to the garden club forty-five minutes early. But when I started to back my car out of the driveway, I got that skittish feeling and knew I had forgotten something.

I searched within my cranium and eventually realized that I'd forgotten to water some marigold seedlings in my greenhouse. It was going to get very warm that day, so I couldn't neglect them, especially since they were destined for a Storytime Garden outside the library where I worked.

I turned off the car, trudged into the house, and entered the greenhouse by way of the sliding glass doors of our den. I began watering the seedlings, but had an odd feeling that someone or something was watching me. I searched around the greenhouse and finally saw two very tiny, beady eyes staring directly at me.

The eyes belonged to a wren, which, outside of a hummingbird, is the smallest bird that visits my garden. Normally, when I'm outside, I don't care if a bird comes by for a chat. But when I'm indoors, birds take on the ominous size and menace of a hungry pterodactyl.

I stealthily propped open the greenhouse door to the backyard, hoping my visitor would leave. Then I went back into the greenhouse and stood next to the sliding glass door to my home.

I froze, and for what seemed like hours, we eyed one another like two gunslingers on a dusty street in Tombstone, Arizona. The bird perched three feet away on a growing bench, positioned between the marigolds and me. My mind raced: Dare I try to water the dry marigolds, and what would the bird do if I tried?

We stayed in this ridiculous standoff until the wren made its move and flew directly at my face! I screamed, crashed into a growing bench, and threw my hands up for protection from the wren's claws. Fortunately, the hideous creature veered off, so I quickly fled into the house and slammed the glass door behind me.

My attacker continued to fly into the glass door while I stood near it. So, I retreated further into the house until the bird stopped battering the door.

I could feel time slipping away and didn't know what to do. I needed to go to my lecture, but my marigolds had to be watered.

Looking down at my pants, I noticed that dirt was on them. Undoubtedly, they had become soiled when I ran from the bird and bumped into one of my growing benches. I cursed and went into the house to wipe them down with a wet towel, then used my wife's hair dryer on them.

With any luck, the wren had exited through the door to the outside. I furtively glanced around the greenhouse and saw no sign of the bird; but just as I was about to enter, I noticed that my marigolds were stirring. I stood in horror as I watched my attacker pecking at my marigolds!

Suddenly my anger welled up. Now, I was a parent ready to defend my children at any cost. All my fear disappeared and I charged into the greenhouse, picked up the flat of marigolds that held the wren, and ran outside. But the wren flew off and went back into the greenhouse to the other flat of marigolds. Undaunted, I took the second flat outside and slammed the greenhouse door.

At long last, the wren was outdoors, but it stayed on the flat, pecking at my annuals.

I didn't dare open the outside door to the greenhouse again. So I took the unoccupied flat of marigolds, ran around to the front of the house, went in, and put the flat back into the greenhouse. Then I went outside, grabbed the second flat, and shook off the pesky wren. I darted back to the front door, ran in, and slammed the door behind me.

Finally, after placing both flats on a growing bench, I watered my marigolds in peace. Peering through my greenhouse windows, I was thankful to see my nemesis on the lawn outside.

It had been a hard-fought victory, but I still had a lecture to give. As I backed my car out of the driveway, my brain sent no further feelings of dreadful forgetfulness, so I sped away to my program.

As I stood there, trying to deliver the lecture despite my jangled nerves, I'm sure that more than a few people in my audience thought I was the smoothest, calmest lecturer they'd ever heard.

Yeah, right.

A Tale of Two Towns:
Punxsutawney and Voorhees
-OR-
A Dickens of a Groundhog

January 25th

105 North Burrow
Bastille St.
Punxsutawney, PA 15767

Dear Punxsutawney Phil, alias Chuck Darnay, alias Chuck Evremonde,

February 2nd is approaching, and although it's the best of times for some, it's the worst of times for you. I know that the last thing you need during this season of darkness is some human bothering you just before you go through another Groundhog Day, but it's time to set the record straight. So please, open your peepers long enough to read this tale of woe from a gardener who's ready to put land mines in his garden.

When I was a kid, I read a short story about wild boars that had turned the tables on a group of hunters and killed most of them. It seemed that these beasts had all the collective animosity of their slaughtered predecessors and took revenge on this one hunting group.

The tale had receded into the foggy areas of my mind until last Groundhog Day. After years of abuse, I finally realized last February 2nd that I'm the one who's been singled out for retribution by the world's woodchucks. But before another Groundhog Day passes, I have to clear my good name. Please believe me when I say that if any person understands the horror of your plight and the idiocy of my fellow humans, it's me.

Let's see if I have it right:

Technologically advanced countries have sent up satellites to track weather systems. We can now discover budding hurricanes when they're mere vapors over the Eastern Atlantic Ocean. We can detect minuscule temperature changes in the waters of the Eastern Pacific Ocean and use them to predict weather patterns for a year. And we can predict, almost to the minute, when a cold front will hit. But in spite of this wizardry, we wake you from your hibernation to give us a six-week forecast.

On February 2nd, thousands of carousing humans gather in your hometown. The scene is not unlike the madness in the streets of revolutionary Paris during the 1790s. The citizens torture you during the middle of your winter sleep. They flash their cameras; they yell and hoot; then they use our sophisticated technological resources to send "your" weather forecast throughout the Northern Hemisphere. And this prognostication is based on whether you've opened your eyes and seen your shadow?

All I can say is, where are all the animal rights activists? At least minks used for fur coats get a full night's sleep. You'd better believe that if thousands of people woke me up in the middle of the night for anything except a flower show, I'd be plotting revenge just like the boars at the front-end of this letter.

So, please understand: I've never, ever, taken part in these ridiculous, raucous rites in Punxsutawney. Despite this, you've sent a message to the world's woodchucks that they should focus their retribution on me.

I live about two hundred yards from high-tension wires. The underlying area can't be developed, so it's the perfect breeding ground for woodchucks. There's a stream for water, tall grass for cover, and a short walk to my garden.

My backyard has a large shed that sits eight inches aboveground. There's a wooden fence around the entire yard. And, since I'm an organic gardener, there's delectable white Dutch clover intermingled throughout our back lawn. The only thing missing is a sign that says, "Rent-Controlled Groundhog Haven."

My garden is the perfect place to grow prize-winning woodchucks.

They're so big, that they would be ideal subjects for a 1950s-style science fiction movie — something like "Attack of the Chernobyl Groundhogs."

The first year that I started my garden, everything was going fine until mid-July. That's when I saw your friend Jacques One in my backyard. In the beginning he dined on clover, so I wasn't unduly alarmed.

But one morning I checked on some ripening tomatoes, and the blood drained from my face when I saw that three had been bitten. I also discovered that my new garden resident was using my shed as a hideout, and that he made frequent trips under my fence and across the street. Although he looked like an ungainly creature, Jacques could run fast. No matter how quickly I moved, I found that I could never come between him and my shed.

After he had sampled more tomatoes and some of my marigolds, I decided I had to use new tactics. I called the local animal shelter and was told to make up a concoction of water, garlic, red pepper, and a few other strong spices to spray under the shed. I chopped, cut, mixed, and sprayed, but found that this supposed remedy had absolutely no effect. Obviously, Jacques had developed his food preferences at a Tex-Mex vegetable garden.

About the time that he had started to give me nightmares, I came out one morning and noticed a groundhog roadkill outside my back fence. Apparently, the steady smorgasbord had weighed him down too much to avoid cars. But although I had survived round one against you and your buddies, more battles were to come. To paraphrase Winston Churchill: It was not the beginning of the end, but only the end of the beginning.

The following year, I started to see evidence of another woodchuck by mid-June, but I wasn't about to let things get out of hand again. I phoned a licensed animal control company that sent an employee, named John, to set up a humane trap near my vegetable patch.*

The next morning, I looked out my window and saw that the trap door was closed. What a relief! Jacques Two had been caught in just one day. I went outside and slowly approached the cage. But wait ... something was wrong. This animal was the size of a groundhog, but

---

*Only licensed companies in New Jersey are permitted to trap and remove live wildlife. I chose one that was known for its humane treatment of animals.

was black ... with a white stripe down its back. It was a skunk; namely your emissary from Paris, Pennsylvania: The Vengeance!

She stared at me with those baleful black eyes, while I was as motionless as a gravestone, certain she'd lift her tail and send a "Rain of Terror" upon me.

After a long wait, I stealthily moved away, then spewed a stream of obscenities as I raced inside. I phoned John, who laughed and told me that since the skunk's tail was down, I wasn't in immediate danger. An hour later, he reset another trap, then took The Vengeance away without her leaving a pungent calling card.

The next day, your friend, Jacques Two, was captured and removed, and I spent the remainder of the summer in blissful peace.

Two years later, a garden club was coming to tour my garden, so I wanted it to look pristine. All summer long I was at war with your friends, but John managed to bag all seven of them before they destroyed my backyard.

After six years and fifteen Jacques later, it's time for us to call a truce. I'm tired of my backyard becoming the place where "Human Day" is celebrated every August 2nd, which just happens to be exactly six months after the day when you're tortured every year. Are your buddies looking to see if I cast a shadow when I'm screaming at the top of my lungs because of their latest feast? And exactly what am I forecasting, the number of weeks until the first frost?

So let's make a deal. I've been talking to some friends at the Movieworld Animatronics Laboratories. They've produced a mechanical groundhog named Sidney, who can act just as sleepy as you every February 2nd. What I'm saying is, if you call off your army of groundhogs, I'll relieve you from your mid-winter torment.

On the night of February 1st, I'll come and whisk you away to new digs in London, Pennsylvania. In your place, Sidney will be ready to endure all the torture that my fellow humans will inflict.

On February 2nd the unsuspecting, carousing crowd will pick up the fake, self-sacrificing groundhog, point a camera and microphone at him and, for the first time in recorded history, a groundhog will speak English. On every television and radio in the United States these words will be heard: "It is a far, far, better thing I do than I have ever done; it is a far, far, better rest that I go to than I have ever known."

If you agree to my plan, I'll even throw in a mate for you named Lucie who'll be with you during your escape. So, for the sake of your sanity and mine, let's end our winter of despair by coming together in the true spirit of friendship. Forevermore our mutual act of freedom will be remembered with the words, "Liberte, Egalite, Fraternite."

Votre ami,

Citizen Wolk

P.S. If you agree to follow my scheme, perhaps we could get together for lunch … but in someone else's garden.*

---

*Although this is a fictionalized account of events that took place in my backyard, towns named London and Paris really exists in Pennsylvania, both within a two-hour drive of Punxsutawney.

Bonkers Over Bunnies

I had every gardener's dream: a backyard that was critter-free. After many years of torment by groundhogs and chipmunks, John, my licensed animal control expert, had caught the marauders that had been making my life a misery.

So, I assumed that that 1997 was going to be a banner gardening year. I drew a design for my flower garden, then started growing annuals from seed. Above all else, I was not going to let any four-legged vegetarians get the best of me.

In May and early June my plants were growing well, but by the end of June, I noticed that my marigolds were being eaten. I mistakenly assumed a groundhog was doing the damage, but within a day, I noticed that a baby rabbit was the culprit. Non-gardeners would have considered it the sweetest, fluffiest creature in the universe. Of course, I viewed it the same way a shepherd views a mountain lion.

At first, I tried to catch it using a large plastic flowerpot, but the bunny always ran under some delicate flowering plant that I wouldn't harm. Feeling stymied, I called John and he baited a trap with lettuce, carrots, and apples — all to no avail.

Next, I started watching the bunny's eating habits and found that, aside from my marigolds, it feasted on plantain and a few other lawn weeds. So I added some of these fresh greens to the trap, but day after day it remained empty. Finally, it dawned on me that if I were a rabbit I wouldn't go near a trap containing limp looking lettuce or carrots when I had a cornucopia of fresh vegetables in "Farmer Wolk's" garden.

My frustration mounted as my marigolds started to resemble botanical anorexics. Feeling desperate, I decided to try to rouse the bunny from its usual haunt — inside a large group of coneflowers — and chase it into some chicken wire fencing.

This plan worked perfectly, except that when the bunny bumped into the fence it simply backed up and went right through it. I've since come to the realization that (1) the holes in my fencing were too large, and (2) bunnies are made of 98% fluff and 2% marigolds.

Next, I decided to gather information about my enemy to figure out how to catch it. I learned that my local rabbits were eastern cottontails (*Sylvilagus floridanus*), and that they're native to virtually the entire United States east of the Rocky Mountains. What's most interesting is their reproductive ability: a female usually has four litters per year with an average of five young per litter. Even more disturbing is the fact that females born in early spring can begin breeding by late summer.

This information left me with three thoughts:

- First: Given their propagation rate, it's no wonder that rabbits can reach a high population so quickly.
- Second: Thank goodness people don't reproduce so quickly, or the earth would have reached the limits of human population long before I was born.
- And third: I needed to act quickly or I would soon have a garden of fur instead of flowers.

Additional research revealed that foxes are a major predator of rabbits and that fox urine is supposed to scare them away. When I visited a local garden center that stocked urine repellants, I found a cornucopia of the stuff, including not just fox, but also bobcat and coyote urine.

Armed and ready for biological warfare, I discharged the brown fox urine into tiny scent bottles that were hung throughout my flower garden. The stuff smelled so vile that I could barely accomplish the task, but I assumed that finally my rabbit would leave the area.

However, my marigolds became thinner and thinner over the next week. So although the awful stuff worked on me because *I* couldn't stand the smell and *I* wanted to leave the garden, my rabbit wouldn't have cared if I flooded the entire flowerbed with fox urine.

Next, I sought advice from local experts. I asked one very experienced employee at a garden center what I could do to get rid of bunnies.

Her response was, "Plant marigolds around the perimeter of your yard. That'll keep them away!"

I thanked her and turned away in disbelief. I was losing more and more marigold foliage every day, and my "expert" was telling me to use marigolds to scare off bunnies.

My next stop was at the door of a friend who was an animal control officer. Finally I was asking a real expert — someone with nineteen years of experience in controlling offensive critters. His response to my query was, "Plant marigolds around the perimeter of your yard. That'll keep them away!"

Now my blood was really boiling. I didn't have the heart to shoot my enemy, and it seemed that no one knew how to get rid of rabbits that were already inside your yard.

I was almost ready to give up on my flower garden, but decided to continue adding fresh greens to John's trap. Then I made a disheartening discovery: I noticed that I hadn't been fighting one bunny all along, but twins that had come out from hiding one at a time. So now I had to trick two rabbits, not one.

The blessed event that finally enabled me to catch my garden marauders was the same event that made every other gardener in my area curse the summer of 1997, namely the July drought.

Earlier in the summer, I couldn't entice the bunnies into John's trap with lettuce, carrots, fresh garden greens, or apples. But when the hot, dry weather hit, the heat and lack of moisture made the apples a commodity for which the bunnies would risk capture. And capture is what I did — both of them.

John took them both away, and, at long last, my marigolds started to put foliage on their bony stems.

Looking back, there's just one thing that worries me and one question that needs answering. I'm worried because I had become so frazzled that summer that I got skittish at the very sight of rabbits. In my mind, they were as frightening as grizzly bears. So my question is, do you suppose my medical insurance company will pay for psychotherapy to correct post-traumatic pest disorder?

"But if you put it in the ground...
won't it get dirty?"

3

GARDEN CLUBS
AND SOCIETIES

A Garden Club Is a Gardening Club ...
Or Is It?

BACK IN THE 1970S, BEFORE I JOINED a garden club, I fantasized that these groups were alike and that they'd consist of the following types of members:

- people who grow a wide variety of plants;
- people who love gardening, including digging in the soil;
- people who would only take credit for plants they grow themselves;
- people who are willing to listen to other growers' gardening techniques; and
- people who want to open their club to as many members as possible.

Of course, the first garden club I joined dashed the first of these fantasies. It was a chrysanthemum society and included many people who grew only mums. All year long, mums were the center of their gardening world: no veggies, no roses, and no bulbs — just mums.

Don't misunderstand me; I think chrysanthemums are wonderful. When you go to a mum show with all the cascades, standards, bonsais, huge incurves, spiders, spoons, and pompons, it can be a veritable assault on the senses.

But why limit yourself to just one genus? Do these same people eat only at one restaurant, read books by only one author, or only see Robert DeNiro's films? I have to admit that I'm with the French: vive la différence!

The next group I joined was an organic gardeners' club in Pennsylvania. It was an ideal choice, because the members and I had the same beliefs about protecting the planet through environment-friendly gardening. But if I thought that I was going to be the most ardent organic gardener, I was very mistaken, since there were members who absolutely lived and breathed organic gardening.

I've been a garden lecturer for many years and have seen about seventy-five clubs in action. Of them all, the gatherings of that organic gardening club came the closest to being revival meetings, and woe betide speakers who didn't follow the creed.

Although the club members were some of the sweetest and dearest people you'd ever meet, sometimes their fervency boiled over. I can remember one lecturer who mentioned that he used an inorganic fertilizer, which prompted one member to shout, "We don't use that stuff!" It not only cast a pall on the meeting, but perhaps on the speaker. Shortly after that program, he stopped lecturing altogether!

Usually I can be pretty fast on my feet when I give lectures, but one ritzy club in New York stumped me. In retrospect, I should have realized something was amiss when one member showed up in a tennis skirt and several others came in expensive suits.

My program was a workshop on bulb forcing, during which the participants potted bulbs and were told to take the pots home and bury them in their gardens. At the end of my lecture, the program chairperson told me that she had received numerous complaints from members about having to go out and dig in their gardens!

It was the first time I realized that some garden clubs are really social clubs masquerading as garden clubs.

Many garden clubs have their own flower shows or have members who participate in the flower shows of other organizations. When I first got the itch to enter these shows, I assumed that horticultural exhibitors were similar to artists who exhibit their sculptures and paintings. I thought that what each flower show exhibitor was saying to the world was, "Look at this beautiful thing that I slaved over, worried about, and groomed so that you could appreciate my accomplishment."

Then, at one flower show, I found out I was wrong. The judges had given a top award to a local celebrity for a pot of forced bulbs. But standing next to the pot was a woman with a big grin who, it turned out, was hired by the celebrity to force the bulbs into bloom. She received no credit for growing the entry, while the celebrity got all the accolades.*

Finally, when I was president of a garden club, I tried to steer the group in the direction that the membership chose. According to my surveys, they wanted to have more members so we could have enough funds to have great programs, visit enthralling gardens, and have a wide range of experience among our membership. And I thought that every garden club would want the same thing.

But I was wrong.

One year, I visited a New Jersey garden club that paid me a hefty fee, but had only forty members at my program. I knew that exactly forty showed up because an oral roll call was taken.

After my program, I learned that the club was limited to forty people because lunch was served by the member who hosted that month's meeting. The membership agreed that it would be too difficult for one member to serve lunch to more than forty people, so the group was limited to that number. They took roll, because if any members missed too many meetings, they were dropped so others could join.

So, in the case of that garden club's membership, the controlling factor was lunch, not gardening.

Coincidentally, the garden club of which I was president had delectable desserts at the end of our meetings. As I mentioned, I surveyed the membership every year to determine their priorities, but I never came close to asking if there was a correlation between their attendance and the quality of our food.

In the end, I decided to hold on to my fantasy that gardening was our primary focus.

---

*See "ghost growers," "non-gardening 'gardeners'," and "name acclaim" in *Flower Show Jargon,* beginning on page 55. Also see *Non-Gardening Gardeners* on page 101.

Killer Questions at Gardening Lectures

Since giving my first gardening lecture in 1990, I've given about 150 programs to a wide variety of garden clubs and societies. In most cases, I don't know anyone in the audience; so to develop rapport, I have to become friendly from the start. It's not unlike evangelists who come into town for one day and not only have to get people to listen to them, but to convert the audience to their firmly held views.

Converting an audience to my horticultural convictions may be asking too much. In fact, while lecturing to some stony-faced crowds, I sometimes consider the program a success if the audience simply stays awake. I always try to add humor to keep their attention. And I encourage questions from the start, because if the audience doesn't understand the easy concepts in the beginning, I'll be drowned out by snoring within twenty minutes.

What I find astounding is that regardless of the setting or time restraints, certain core questions are always asked. Here are the most common ones:

1. "What can I do about the deer that are ravaging the plants in my backyard?"

This is *the* most asked question by audiences at gardening programs in my area. What's incredible is that the lecture topic doesn't matter in the least.

I can remember giving one lecture about preparing plants for flower shows. When I finished, the first question from the audience was, "What can I do about deer?" I got the feeling that the questioner went through agony, holding herself back from blurting out the question while I expounded on topiaries, houseplants, and potted bulbs. At long last, she opened the floodgates.

Unfortunately, this topic seems to be cathartic for most audiences: suddenly, everyone offers solutions. And, while this keeps everyone awake, it tends to move us almost irreversibly away from the topic at hand. It takes all of my talent as a speaker to halt the tidal wave of anti-deer sentiment and return to the original subject.

Even so, I'm fascinated by the measures that gardeners use to keep deer away from their plants. Although this isn't a "how-to" book, I can't resist sharing this gem: A woman at one of my lectures said that the best method for keeping deer away was to hang her underwear around the perimeter of the garden. And, it was especially important that it be *dirty* underwear. I am not endorsing this method, since I don't have problems with deer and therefore haven't tested it. But it gets my "Creativity Award." Of every gardening technique I've ever learned, this one is way, way at the top of the list for originality.

2. "Why is my plant dying?"

This question ranks barely below the deer question. Sometimes, people who ask this question don't know the name of their plant, and usually the only symptom mentioned is that their "plant looks sick." Interestingly, although they probably would never think of having a doctor diagnose their illness without an exam, the questioner never, ever, brings the sickly plant for me to scrutinize.

All I can do is give a best "guesstimate" and hope that if my suggestion doesn't work, I don't get the dead plant sent to me in the mail.

3. "What plant is a perennial that blooms in deep shade from spring until fall?"

This is another question that gets asked regardless of the topic of the lecture. It even gets asked if I'm talking about annuals for sunny gardens.

Of course, it's a trick question because no such plant exists. The questioner is either trying to make me stumble or they're searching for the botanical version of Superman. The best response is to offer my phone number and ask the questioner to call me when they find the answer.

What's especially interesting about these "Black Forest" gardeners is that they look at me as if I'm a serial killer when I suggest that they cut down a few trees for sunlight to have the high-impact flower garden of their dreams.

4. "Could you please design a garden for me before you leave?"

This one doesn't get asked until after the formal part of the lecture is over. I'm usually packing up my paraphernalia when someone ambushes me with a blank sheet of paper and asks the killer question of the night.

I have a friend who's a landscape architect, and he takes weeks or even months to do what my interrogator wants me to do in five minutes. With this kind of question, the only answer is to suggest landscape design books or landscape architects. But there's always one alternative: I can call home and tell my wife that I'll be delayed until Halley's Comet reappears.

5. "I've planted sunflowers in the same spot for five years, but this year they look lousy. What did I do wrong?"

This is another question that's right up there with "Why is my plant dying?"

Invariably, these gardeners have gone through the pain of having productive gardens one year that turn into veritable dust bowls the next. They spend big bucks on trees, shrubs, and bedding plants, then watch them all die one by one.

The problem is that although their soil is the canvas on which they paint their landscape, it's not the lifeless canvas used by artists. So, I explain that soil has particles of varying sizes, from microscopic clay to coarse sand to boulders. It also has macronutrients (i.e., nitrogen, phosphorus, and potassium), micronutrients (e.g., boron, iron, and sulfur), and organic matter. Further, I tell them that these are all mixed together in infinite combinations all over the globe; and, at any one place, they vary from year to year and even season to season.

Then I suggest that they do what all the world's best gardeners and farmers do: get a soil test. But sad to say, explaining the secrets of soil is dangerous territory for any garden lecturer. Usually you get cloned blank stares, which tell you that you've sent your audience somewhere between "La-La" land and the Land of Oz.

Fortunately, this speaker-induced catatonia has an instant cure: Just say the word "money" and the trance is broken. I usually mention that in order protect their $500 investment in nursery stock, they should spend $10 on a soil test done by their county agricultural extension agents. In return for their investment, I tell them that they'll get a personalized letter about their soil and what it needs to make it a hospitable place for plants.

I'm always gratified by the looks I get when this message sinks in. I swear, it's the closest that my lectures ever come to being revival meetings. And I never feel more empowered than at that moment — I've got the entire group in the grip of my garden gloves.

So I leave elated, thinking they'll all contact their agricultural extension agents to get soil tests. But, by the time I wake up the next day, I'm sure that the odds of my audience's county agents receiving a lot more soil samples are about equal to my chances of taking the helm of a nuclear submarine.

Finally, although I try my best, I may not be able to give gardeners the exact answers they want. On the other hand, the check they give me is the exact answer to the question of how I'll pay my monthly mortgage.

4

FLOWER SHOWS
PART ONE

Flower Show Jargon

MAJOR FLOWER SHOWS, LIKE THE one that takes place in Philadelphia, are a world unto themselves — filled with plants, exhibitors, judges and other people and paraphernalia. The following flower show glossary will help you understand terms freely used in this chapter as well as in Chapter 8.

exhibitors: Gardeners who prefer blue ribbons over blue diamonds. Most horticultural exhibitors buy plants based solely on the probability of their winning a blue ribbon. During the Philadelphia Flower Show, exhibitors are on a natural high that lasts for at least nine days; then they're completely exhausted for at least ninety. When purchasing plants listed in a catalog, these gardeners mainly look at the description of the plant, and barely glance at the price.

non-exhibiting gardeners: Gardeners who visit flower shows, but don't have the faintest idea why exhibitors drive themselves so hard. They think blue nylon is blue nylon and nothing more. They also think most experienced exhibitors are well on their way to becoming demented.

ghost growers: These are the angels who walk around on earth masquerading as humans. They're usually hired by wealthy, non-gardening "gardeners" to grow plants entered in the name of their employer at major flower shows.

non-gardening "gardeners":
People who don't grow a single plant entered in their name at major flower shows, but who get all the "name acclaim" (see page 58).

passers: Made up mainly of volunteers, this group consists of amateur and professional horticulturists who decide whether an exhibit or plant is worthy of entry into a flower show. They make sure that the plants contain no pests and aren't diseased. Virtually all of them have been exhibitors in the past and understand the stress that many exhibitors "exhibit." They also make helpful suggestions to entrants so that the exhibitor's plants have a better chance of receiving blue ribbons. In Philadelphia Flower Show terminology, once a plant has been given the OK from passers, it is said to be "passed."

judges: The umpires of flower shows who are treated exactly like their baseball brethren. They work hard to be as fair as possible in handing out awards. Exhibitors rarely, if ever, thank a judge when they receive a blue ribbon, because they think their plant was the obvious

There are three types of flower show entries:

• Horticultural entries-
consist of any plant or plants grown in a container: from miniatures grown in 3" pots, to those larger than a sumo wrestler. There are also topiaries consisting of huge numbers of small plants grown over an animal-shaped metal frame (e.g., a fifteen-foot-tall giraffe).

• Artistic entries-
can be as small as a 5" dried-flower arrangement or as large as a decorated room, but regardless of size, they must contain living or dried plants. Judges use the principles and elements of design to decide which entries are worthy of ribbons. At the Philadelphia Flower Show, some artistic entries — especially the pressed plant pictures — are so awe-inspiring that they belong in art museums.

• Major entries-
are of two varieties: (1) those that resemble entire landscaped gardens, and (2) those that could pass for reception rooms at royal weddings.

Regardless of the types of entries, all exhibitors give them the amount of attention that could only be compared with that conferred upon seventeenth century European nobility.

choice. On the other hand, exhibitors who don't receive a blue ribbon angrily blame the judges, because they "mis"judged their entry. Smart judges never identify themselves to irate exhibitors; for safety's sake, they're more likely to disappear into a crowd.

bulb forcing: Perhaps bulb coaxing, persuading, or imploring would be more accurate terms. Spring-blooming bulbs — like tulips, daffodils, and hyacinths — are planted in pots, chilled, and brought indoors so that they bloom weeks or even months ahead of outdoor bulbs.* While indoors, the flowers are at their peak for less than twenty-four hours, so exhibitors do everything they can to make the peak hours occur during judging. Unfortunately, what often happens is that exhibitors have breathtaking flower shows at home, a week too soon or too late. In such cases, exhibitors not only lose blue ribbons, but hair, peace-of-mind, and the capability of holding a simple conversation.

double-layered bulbs: Containerized overpopulation that involves planting twice the usual number of spring-blooming bulbs in a pot. The first layer of bulbs is planted on potting mix halfway up the pot, more mix is added, then a second layer of bulbs is planted and covered with soil. Theoretically, this produces pots with twice the number of flowers, thus doubling the chances of winning blue ribbons.[†] But getting all the forced bulbs to bloom at the same time involves not just horticultural ability, but tremendous luck. Of course, doubling the bulb-count also means that the cost per pot doubles. But exhibitors ignore this because the possibility of winning a blue ribbon suspends all fiscal propriety.

---

*Most spring-blooming bulbs require cool conditions for root formation and flower stem extension. Bulbs are subjected to cool temperatures (40-48°F) for 10-14 weeks, then brought indoors. To produce the proper temperature range, potted bulbs are either buried in the ground or placed in refrigerators or cold frames. (See foonote on cold frames, page 29.)

[†]High flower count can so bedazzle judges that they miss otherwise noticeable imperfections. Virtually every bulb exhibitor I know agrees that this happens ... especially if a blue ribbon is clipped to an "Art Wolk" entry card.

blues: Non-gardeners think this word refers to sad songs with lyrics about lost loves, lost trains, lost trucks, or lost dogs. To flower show exhibitors, "blues" are blue ribbons. If they're won, the exhibitor doesn't lose anything, but gains pride, respect, ecstasy, satisfaction, as well as envy from other competitors.

other awards: Aside from blues, there are other ribbons, namely, those that are red (2nd place), yellow (3rd place), or white (honorable mention). Experienced exhibitors really consider the latter a "dishonorable" mention award. There are also fancy, frilled ribbons, called rosettes, awarded to the best of the blue ribbon entries in a variety of plant categories. For example, the Delaware Valley Daffodil Society rosette is awarded to the best of approximately eight daffodil entries that each won a blue ribbon that day.

At the Philadelphia Flower Show, each ribbon is worth a certain number of points, with blue ribbons having the highest value. Exhibitors who accumulate enough points can win three different silver sweepstakes trophies for entries in (1) the horticultural classes, (2) the artistic classes, or (3) the horticultural and artistic classes combined. The latter is named the Grand Sweepstakes Award; but a more suitable name, when won by the author of this book, would be the Grand Obsessive-Compulsive, Drive-Your-Family-Nuts Award.

name acclaim: At flower shows, these are the names posted next to blue ribbons or engraved on trophies, regardless of whether the people with those names grew the plants.

visitors: The neck-craning crowd divided into two populations:
- **gardeners**: People who have so much cabin fever in late winter, that they'd visit a flower show even if it contained just one potted plant. Of course, what's really present at major flower shows are thousands of potted plants and entire landscaped gardens. After standing in long lines to see each display, they do not, in any way, notice that time has passed.
- **non-gardeners**: People who feel that they've been plunked into the middle of a Times Square New Year's Eve celebration. They

look at their watches more than the flowers, and continuously tell the time to the gardener who dragged them there. For some reason, the gardener has selective perception and doesn't notice a single entreaty from the non-gardener. When the visit finally ends, non-gardeners promise themselves never to go to a flower show again. On the other hand, they just might relent if their gardening friend promised to give them $5 million in a numbered Swiss bank account.

My First Blue Ribbon
-OR-
Are You Sure You've Got the Name Right?

Is there anything as sweet, innocent, and breathtaking as the first kiss from our first love? It stirs the soul and is never forgotten. That kiss is one of those rare stitches that are sewn forever into the fabric of our memory: frozen in time, always savored, always remembered, regardless of our age.

For participants at major flower shows, their first blue ribbon comes very close to that first kiss, except that memory isn't the only thing that's frozen: our entire bodies are frozen as well. We stand there like statues, mouths agape and feet immovable, with all the signs of rigor mortis. One's brain, quite simply, rejects the possibility of winning a blue ribbon. Normally it takes fractions of a second for the brain to process something as small as eight square inches of colored fabric. However, for these eight square inches of blue nylon, the brain doesn't accept this fact for about three days.

Here's how I got mine:

I was living in a one-bedroom apartment with my wife, and had become smitten with plants. I had terrariums on tables, philodendron draped around curtains, and assorted botanical detritus everywhere. My wife brought the first plant into our home — an event she still regrets: I was bit by the gardening bug and have yet to recover.

In 1978 we visited the Philadelphia Flower Show for the first time. I was entranced by the immense and imaginative major displays. But there was also an area called the Horticourt, where amateurs and professionals competed in hundreds of different plant categories for blue, red, yellow, and white ribbons.

I was impressed, but not intimidated. That flower show planted a competitive spirit in me that exists to this day.

In the fall of 1978, I obtained an exhibitor's booklet from the Pennsylvania Horticultural Society (PHS) and learned about the variety of competitive classes. I decided to enter forced bulbs as well as a Ming aralia (*Polyscias fruticosa*) that I had been shaping for two years into a gently, downward swirling beauty. With great anticipation, I sent the required list of plants I intended to exhibit to the PHS.

During the Philadelphia Flower Show, which takes place the first week in March, there are three different days (Saturday, Tuesday, and Friday) when plants can be entered and judged. We had other plans for the first Saturday, so I aimed my Ming aralia for Tuesday and my potted bulbs for Friday.

I spent an hour grooming the aralia on Monday evening: removing dead leaves, cleaning the healthy ones, and pruning it into the exact shape I wanted. Since exhibitors only have from seven to nine-thirty in the morning to get their pots passed for entry into the show, I got an early start on Tuesday morning. After gently loading the aralia into my car, I drove to Philadelphia's Civic Center, got my plant entered, and went to work in downtown Philadelphia.

I knew that by three o'clock the judging results would be recorded, so I spent the entire day clock-watching. After suffering through hours of torment, the hour hand on the clock finally pointed at "3."

I immediately called the Flower Show office and asked for the results of the class I had entered.* The woman who answered, flipped through a stack of papers, and eventually said, "Blue ribbon to Art Wolk, red ribbon to ..."

My mind froze.

Eventually, I stopped her recitation and said, "Are you sure you've got the name right? Blue ribbon to Art Wolk?" She said yes, that was the name on the results sheet. I blurted out that she could stop, because that was my name. She congratulated me and I very slowly hung up the phone.

I don't think I moved for a full minute. When I came out of my stupor, I floated back to my cubicle, mentioning my news to a few friends.

---

*There are more than 150 horticultural competitive classes during the week of the Philadelphia Flower Show. My aralia was in the category "Plants Grown in the House."

Those who were gardeners gave me hearty congratulations; non-gardeners greeted my news as if they were on a general anesthetic.

A big part of me didn't believe the lady on the phone. So after work, I went to the show, rushed through the crowd, and finally saw my plant. And, there it was: a blue ribbon stapled to an entry card that displayed my name.

I stood there exactly like all my predicessors: slack-jawed and inanimate. If someone had thrown a lit match into my mouth, I don't think I would have noticed.

Then the fun started. Hundreds, if not thousands, of people went past my plant, and I heard positive comments from them that made me feel like royalty. I immodestly thanked many of them. Their responses were identical: "That's your plant? It looks great! You deserved the blue ribbon."

So why are blue ribbons so exciting? After all, they're just flimsy pieces of nylon that couldn't restrain a mouse. But some gardeners slave for years to win their first at a competition like the Philadelphia Flower Show. If won, it causes euphoria so overwhelming, that you feel like you've just broken the bank at Monte Carlo, won the Irish Sweepstakes, as well as a $100 million lottery. One of my friends was reduced to unstoppable tears. Others claim the event is surreal; that one part of them is looking at the ribbon and another is taking in the scene from outside their body.

Exhibitors may have different ways of showing and describing their euphoria, but the overwhelming emotions are universal.

I won other ribbons with my potted bulbs on Friday, but that first blue ribbon had a narcotic effect on me. I was hooked on flower show exhibiting and to this day the barb hasn't been removed. The moment would never be forgotten: It was sweet, innocent, and breathtaking, just like my first kiss.

Why Is That Dark Cloud Following Me?

My friend Todd was following me to the Philadelphia Flower Show, had half my entries in his car, and now he was gone. I had lost him on the bridge that spanned the Delaware River and knew he didn't know how to get to the show. I felt desperate, since I had only 2½ hours to get my potted bulbs entered into the competition. I couldn't ask the police to help; searching for people was one thing, searching for blooming daffodils was another. I could only pray that I'd find Todd and that everything else would go smoothly. But worse was yet to come, both that year and the rest of the odd-numbered years in the 1990s.

These types of nerve-wracking emergencies are common to all Philadelphia Flower Show exhibitors. We grow our plants, gather our supplies, make detailed plans, but it doesn't matter — something always goes wrong. For us, the only unknowns are when our disasters will occur, their severity, and whether we'll have the temperament to withstand them.

On the other side of the emotional spectrum are flower show visitors. They typically come after work, and move along at a relaxed pace while drinking coffee and chatting with friends. It's late winter and the gorgeous indoor panoramas of flowering plants and trees caress their spirits. Very few know that it's taken a year of planning and more than a week and tens of thousands of dollars to create these indoor gardens.

Next, these visitors glance at their watches and notice that it's 8:00PM. They head over to the Horticourt, where individual plant entries look so pristine that the visitors assume they are the result of ideal growing conditions. Surely, they think, the exhibitors have advanced degrees in horticulture and greenhouses with an abiding staff to play nursemaid to the masterpieces they see every year. They also imagine that the exhibition process is a smooth undertaking by well-adjusted, calm adults.

But the truth is that just twelve hours before their visit, the "Show Within The Show" was taking place. The "Show" I'm talking about is composed of highly competitive exhibitors scurrying around like mice running amok after the cage door has been opened. An objective observer would think we've, quite literally, gone over to the "Dark Side."

We bring our plants, seeking ribbons or perhaps silver cups. Most of us do the best we can by growing our entries on a windowsill or under fluorescent lights. So, while we may have the exuberance of botanical researchers, few of us have the same resources. For twelve months, exhibitors have been meticulously growing and grooming plants. On the night before judging, many exhibitors get about three hours of sleep, or perhaps none at all. Then, early the next morning, growers transport their specimens to the show and, on tenterhooks, await the decisions of the judges.

The backdrop for this highly charged atmosphere is a flower show that's the oldest, largest, and, many consider, best in the world.* I've been exhibiting in the Philadelphia Flower Show since 1979 and am proud to be part of it. As I've mentioned before, it's staged by The Pennsylvania Horticultural Society, one of the world's oldest and most prestigious gardening organizations. Back in the 1960s, the Society's president, Ernesta Ballard, decided that along with garden-sized major exhibits, home gardeners should also have a chance to exhibit their potted plants and flower arrangements. So, to this day, home gardeners are still battling for blue ribbons and silver sweepstakes awards. Given our rush of adrenaline, we never feel more alive than during that one week each year.

We come from a variety of professions, backgrounds, and education levels. At the Philadelphia Flower Show, exhibiting becomes a social leveler. Where else can ordinary folk perennially hug and chat with multi-millionaires? But regardless of our backgrounds, we're addicted to the competition and the excitement it engenders.

I'm also caught up in the quest for blue ribbons. At flower show time, I'm like a hummingbird, zipping around at triple speed and spewing out sentences as fast as a bidding-master. I'm not sure how I look to bystanders, but they look like hibernating snails to me.

---

*The Philadelphia Flower Show is the only indoor flower show listed in the well-regarded book, *1,000 Places To See Before You Die*, by Patricia Schultz (New York: Workman Publishing, 2003) 700-1.

Not all Flower Show exhibitors are as frenetic as I. Cactus grow-ers are the calmest, since their plants have been dormant for five months. Spring-blooming bulb exhibitors are their overwrought oppo-sites: We look like we're ready to have an emotional meltdown every ten minutes.

This seems like madness to the average gardener who visits flower shows. After all, we're talking about a quest for blue ribbons, not gold bullion. But I understand the visitor's viewpoint, because there was a time when I was a non-exhibiting gardener. I first forced spring-blooming bulbs at home in 1978, and, when the flowers appeared, I immediately decided that forcing bulbs for the Philadelphia Flower Show would be a lark. Of course, I was delusional. Forcing bulbs for home use, where flowers bloom when they're ready, isn't even distant-ly related to forcing bulbs so that blossoms are at their peak when the judges walk by on a predetermined day.

It's difficult to understand our plight, so here's an apt simile: Imagine being a cook on a train who has to prepare the perfect meal for judges who get on at the end of the line. The ingredients are deliv-ered to you at stops along the way. Your objective is to make every part of the meal come together at exactly the right time. But things happen: Cooking the duck takes less time than usual, the mashed pota-toes are a bit thin, the bread dough isn't rising fast enough, the train is behind schedule, and on, and on it goes. But you persevere, and when the judges taste your meal, they think it's sheer ambrosia. The bread tastes like it came from a French bakery, the mashed potatoes are exquisite, and the braised duck is delectable. They pronounce you a win-ner, but have no idea what you've gone through, trying to summon all your creative energies while, at the same time, fighting a panic attack.

This scenario is similar to what bulb exhibitors go through, except we're on a train that can take five months to get to the judges' station, and we depend on more things going on outside the train, like air tem-perature and sunlight.

Our yearly cycle runs like this: When the Philadelphia Flower Show ends in March, we're completely worn out. It's a bone weary kind of exhaustion that can take weeks or months to erase. We collect our pots on the last Sunday night of the show, and we're so anxious to get home that we usually ignore the flower show "police" who tell us not to remove our pots until seven o'clock. What usually happens is that one frazzled exhibitor takes a pot away around quarter to seven, and this one infraction usually causes frenzy among exhibitors. We have about as much decorum as starved piranha on the attack.

By the time we get home, the one thing we crave is our bed, and the last things we want to see are our bulbs. Many of our pots are shoved into a corner of our gardens and forgotten.

Around July, the new bulb catalogs arrive and the timing is perfect, because it's taken us almost four months to feel refreshed. It's also taken that long to forget about the Flower Show expenses, the judges you cursed, and the promises you made to yourself to cut back on your number of entries. Then comes the clincher: the Flower Show exhibitors' guide arrives. Visions of blue ribbons bewitch you, and the Flower Show's seductive spell takes hold.

Like generals planning a military campaign, bulb growers make lists of daffodils, tulips, crocuses, hyacinths, *Muscari*, *Scilla*, and *Iris*. Then, with credit card in hand, we order our flower show arsenal. The expense mounts up, but that doesn't matter because blue ribbons and glory lie ahead.

In the beginning it seems so simple. Containers are scrubbed, then bulbs are potted-up and chilled underground or in cold frames for approximately three months (see footnote, page 57). One exceptional bulb exhibitor, Walt Fisher, has even built his own walk-in refrigerator for temperature control. I'm no less fastidious, and had an electrician hook up two cold frames with heating cables and refrigeration thermo-stats to control the temperature of the soil under my potted bulbs.

Next comes what I call the "Flower Show Shuffle." Potted bulbs are brought indoors for forcing — a process that can take anywhere from three days to three months, depending on the type of bulb. It seems like a scientific endeavor, but it's really an art form, with quite a bit of magic thrown in. Exhibitors rely on past experience as a guide, but there are so many variables that it's a bit like rolling dice in Las Vegas.

For starters, the same bulb variety, subjected to identical condi-tions, can have different forcing patterns from year to year. Next, if you rely on sunlight during forcing, a series of cloudy days can cause havoc. Even worse, if it's been a warm winter, minor bulbs like *Crocus* or *Iris* start blooming months before the Philadelphia Flower Show.

Larger flowering bulbs, like daffodils and tulips, are just as inconsistent, so you shuffle some outside or into your unheated garage to hold them back.

After 1979, I continued exhibiting in the Philadelphia Flower Show, winning a few more blue ribbons. Then, in 1993, we had an 8' by 13' greenhouse built onto the back of our New Jersey home. For the first time, I was going to enter every bulb category.

In the fall of 1992, I planted bulbs in fifty pots; and, after sufficient time in my cold frames, they were brought into our greenhouse. As the 1993 Philadelphia Flower Show approached, my anxiety started to build. I had at least one helper lined up for the three judging days in the Horticourt. Everything was going smoothly, but deep inside I knew that unforeseen problems would occur.

The first one came five days before the show.

My station wagon started making strange noises, and my mechanic's prognosis couldn't have been worse: The motor was in its death throes. I decided to get a used engine, but it would take almost a week to complete the switch. In the end, I delayed the transplant and limped along in a car that had a maximum speed of 40 mph.

Saturday, March 6th: On the first judging day, I entered twelve pots in the bulb categories and non-bulbous plants in other classes. As mentioned before, exhibitors have from seven to nine-thirty in the morning to get their material groomed and passed. With so much to enter in two-and-a-half hours, my wife, Arlene, and daughter, Beth, helped out.

I was especially anxious to see how a 12" pot of 'Golden Harvest' daffodils would fare. This variety usually yields two flowers per bulb. So, by double-layering these narcissi in the fall, I had given myself a chance to produce a magnificent success ... or complete failure.* In February I watched the leaves and flower stems emerge every day. Unbelievably, they all grew at the same pace. Then, like a fireworks finale, every flower opened two days before the show, producing a pot with seventy blossoms.

At the show, we put each entry on a table reserved for grooming. Arlene, Beth, and I cleaned foliage and blossoms, then worked on the

---

*See "double-layered bulbs," page 57.

clay pots, taking off blemishes with sandpaper. We also spread a thin layer of vegetable oil on the outside of the pots to remove unsightly salt stains. We finished just before the nine-thirty deadline.

Soon the judges took over and worked in relative isolation. Exhibitors were sent to a separate room where everyone crackled with energy, hope, and expectation.

Finally, at half past eleven, we raced to see the results. Scouring the various classes, we found that I had received a number of red (2nd place) and yellow (3rd place) ribbons, but no blues. Fortunately though, the judging wasn't finished. After an interminable hour, I ran to my 'Golden Harvest' daffodils. Sitting next to them, there was not only a blue ribbon, but also a blue rosette for having the best of eight daffodil entries that had earned blue ribbons.*

What a thrill!

I had received blue ribbons before, but never a rosette. There were backslaps and hugs from family and friends. The rest of the day I was in a trance. Receiving a rosette meant that I would be invited to my first awards banquet the following Saturday.

Monday, March 8th: The person who usually helped me enter plants on Tuesdays called to say she couldn't come. I phoned several possible substitutes, but no one was available. I was on my own.

I had twelve entries targeted for a variety of categories, and stayed up until one o'clock grooming them.

Tuesday, March 9th: Up at five o'clock, I loaded the twelve entries into my car and left by seven. I didn't have time to put protective cushioning between the pots; but since I was driving slowly, I thought they'd be safe. I estimated that I'd be at the Civic Center at 7:40AM and have almost two hours to enter everything.

On the road, I made sure to leave enough space between my car and the vehicle in front of me. But as I was passing a high school, a crossing guard ran out and threw his hands up to stop traffic. The car in front screeched to a halt, so I had to do the same. I held my breath and heard pots falling like bowling pins. Before I turned to survey the

---

*There are a variety of competitive classes for daffodil entries. These include several classes in which everyone grows the same type of daffodil, like *Narcissus* 'Ice Follies,' as well as several "open" classes, like "Any Miniature *Narcissus*."

damage, I noticed that the guard had rushed out to help an *empty* school bus leave the parking lot.

Obscenities streamed from my lips as I pulled over and turned around to see the carnage: Several tulip leaves and blossoms were broken, and other plants were jostled and needed major repair. I took twenty minutes to secure everything, then continued.

The time I lost put me squarely in the middle of rush-hour traffic. By the time I got to the Civic Center it was 8:10AM; I had only eighty minutes to get everything repaired and entered. Amid anger and panic, I worked on the tulips, trimming leaves and blossoms at the speed of a military barber. One pot of English daisies, whose stems and blossoms had been perfectly erect two hours before, now looked like scattered pick-up sticks. I worked feverishly, then frantically searched for a passer.

At 9:00 I still had six more pots to enter; at 9:20, three more; at 9:30, one more. Too late!

Suddenly, I felt as if all my energy was gone. The lack of sleep, the flying pots, the limping car, the high-speed chase around the exhibit floor, had all taken their toll. Even the simple task of gathering my supplies seemed overwhelming.

In spite of my mid-trip tragedy, I did well. The pruned tulips got a third. But, I won two more blue ribbons for my grape hyacinths and miniature daffodils. Almost everything else won something. I felt elated, if exhausted.

Wednesday, March 10th: I began setting my sights on Friday's judging. A 12" pot of 'Fortissimo' daffodils appeared to have the best chance for a blue ribbon. Other promising entries included English daisies, hyacinths, miniature daffodils, tulips, and especially a pot of *Scilla* with seventy bulbs crammed inside an 8" pot.

It was cloudy on Wednesday morning, so I turned on the overhead sodium discharge lamps in our greenhouse to nudge a few pots into bloom. At work, I repeatedly phoned my wife, asking her to turn off the lights when the sun came out or turn them on when the clouds returned. The pots already at their peak were placed in our unheated garage or front patio.

Thursday, March 11th: The pot filled with *Scilla* was given a brief shot of sunshine, so that by late afternoon every one of the seventy bulbs had bloomed. When viewed from the top, you couldn't see the pot because the flowers hid everything.

It was perfect.

That night, I groomed twelve pots for Friday's judging. My pot of hyacinths had six good bloom stalks and a seventh that was a little behind. I decided to put the pot directly under our bright, warm dining room chandelier. I finally got to bed at two o'clock in the morning.

Friday, March 12th: Up at five o'clock, I ate and got my supplies ready. My friend Todd arrived at half past six and helped me load my car. The plants were a bit overcrowded, so Todd talked me into putting half my entries into his wagon. He didn't know the way to the Civic Center in Philadelphia, but he agreed to stay close behind me.

Everything went smoothly: no falling pots or suicidal crossing guards. I kept Todd in my rear view mirror, but when we got to the bridge that crossed the Delaware River, he was missing!

I frantically looked left, right, front, and rear, but couldn't find Todd. The line of cars in back of me grew larger. Horns blew. The toll collector glared. I had to go. On the bridge, I looked everywhere, but saw no sign of him. Then, just as I neared the end of the bridge, I spotted Todd in the far right lane. By frantically leaning on my horn I got his attention, and he quickly managed to move three lanes to the left to get behind me.

We got all of the plants into the Civic Center and Todd helped groom both pots and plants. Aside from the fiasco on the bridge, his help was invaluable. As a matter of fact, I was the main cause of problems at this stage. While I was preparing a pot of tulips for entry, I noticed red spots on some leaves. I cleaned the leaves, but a minute later they reappeared. Then I noticed that my right hand was red too.

It was my blood.

Using a razor blade to remove a damaged leaf, I had nicked my finger. Luckily, the blood hadn't clotted, so I quickly wiped it off the leaves, then covered my cut with a band-aid.

Todd and I worked steadily, but by 9:25 I still had one more pot to enter. Since it wasn't in the bulb categories, I had to run to the proper staging area. At 9:28 I was almost at my destination, but two acquaintances were heading toward me to have a chat. I frantically waved them off, and, with thirty seconds to spare, my last pot was passed.

Todd and I collected my scattered materials, parked our cars, and walked around the show while judging commenced. As had happened the previous Saturday, I received a slew of seconds and thirds. The 12" pot of 'Fortissimo' daffodils only got an honorable mention, probably because I didn't have the heart to remove blooms that were too tall. In the world of horticulture, sometimes less is more. Blue ribbons are awarded for pots with blooms of uniform size and height; and, with daffodils, the noses of the blooms should face symmetrically outward. This may sound like slight-of-hand, but you can achieve uniformity if you turn potted daffodils 90° each day.

The biggest disappointment was my pot of *Scilla*, which also received an honorable mention. The blue ribbon went to my friend Ray Rogers for his *Arisaema sikokianum*, a jack-in-the-pulpit plant rarely seen at flower shows. This same plant won three straight blues that week in the "Other Hardy Bulbs" category. I began to realize that judges were less likely to award blue ribbons to entries that were commonplace, even if they looked perfect.

Next, I headed over to the tulips where the judges were carefully considering each entry. But as one clerk chatted with them, she slipped and appeared to fall in slow motion. Although her nosedive seemed to go on forever, I found that I couldn't move to help her. The shock of what was happening kept me stuck in place while she fell, and sat, directly on top of my pot of tulips!

Everyone descended around the clerk to help her get up. Once she was vertical, my eyes and mouth widened when I noticed them trying to prop up my tulips that had suddenly developed mid-stem joints. Seeing my contorted tulips was more than I could bear; I turned on my heels and fled. After five minutes, I cooled down and returned to find that my pot of broken tulips had been left in the show. Luckily, I found some sympathetic passers who agreed to remove them.

The wrecked tulips and my lack of a blue ribbon left me feeling deflated, but as I prepared to leave, I remembered my pot of cowslips (*Primula veris*). They had won a second in the primrose category on Tuesday, and on Friday I entered them, almost as an afterthought — and without any grooming — in the "Herbaceous Hardy Perennial" category. To my astonishment, it had won a blue ribbon.

My gloom disappeared and the earlier disaster was forgotten. It seemed as if that one day had mirrored the events of the entire growing year: ups and downs, failures and successes, and the definite need for a sense of humor.

My final count for the week was one major award, four blue ribbons, nine seconds, eight thirds, and five honorable mentions. I had garnered enough points to be in eighth place overall. It had been my most successful flower show and the awards banquet was yet to come.

Saturday, March 13th: If this date in 1993 sounds familiar, it's because one of the worst blizzards in weather history occurred that day on the United States East Coast. In the morning, I called the Philadelphia Flower Show office and learned that the awards banquet was still scheduled to take place. I didn't know if I'd ever qualify again, so I was determined to go. After dressing like a North Pole researcher, I shoveled my way to my wife's car and did a steady 18 mph all the way in.

On a Saturday when attendance usually reached 25,000, only 641 hearty souls came, and it seemed as if less than one-tenth that number were there. In spite of the storm, most of us were upbeat, with universal grins that could be translated as, "This is the worst storm of the century and we really don't give a damn, because flower shows come first."

Unfortunately, Ray Rogers, who had worked so hard and had entered so many stunning plants, couldn't come from Northern New Jersey to receive his Horticultural Sweepstakes Award. He had earned almost three times as many points as the exhibitor in second place. The previous day he told me "Wild horses couldn't keep [him] away."

Wild storms were another matter.

So why do we do it? While I may be an extreme case, most exhibitors go through the same anguish, worry, stress, and occasional glee. To us, exhibiting is an unquenchable addiction.

After the storm, Rogers told me that he, "wouldn't push [himself] to win the Horticultural Sweepstakes in the future: It was too exhausting and time consuming." I understood his reasoning, but virtually all of us say the same thing on the last day of the flower show, then enter as many, if not more, plants the next year.

Of course, my quest was to win as many blue ribbons as possible, and Rogers certainly stood between me and those ribbons. But I also realized how important it was for exhibitors like him to stay active in the Philadelphia Flower Show. Just as Jack Nicklaus and Tiger Woods pushed golfers to greater excellence, Rogers did the same for us. By successfully exhibiting plants that were rare and difficult to grow, he forced us to expand our horticultural horizons. So in the end, I told him, "Stick around Ray, we need you."

After a few weeks, I thought that at the next show, I might try to grow an *Arisaema* like Ray's. But I also thought that maybe, just maybe, if I got eighty *Scilla* bulbs into one 8" pot, I just might deny him one more blue ribbon.

It's the same for all flower show exhibitors: dreams keep the competitive fires burning.

"I should be back in 3 days dear...only 152 more
'extra' seedlings that need homes."

5

ONE GARDENER'S
OPINIONS

Thin Seedlings?
Perish the Thought!

WHILE THE WORLD AT LARGE WRESTLES with the problems caused by human overpopulation, the world "at small" — meaning each gardener — grapples with the difficulties caused by backyard botanical overpopulation.

Here's the conundrum to which I refer: Gardeners get a seed packet that states that the germination rate will be 98% for the 200 seeds it contains. We ignore this information and decide that we'll get 4% germination, so we sow every single one of the seeds. One week later, we've got 196 seedlings for an intended area of four square feet. Eight seedlings would probably be enough, so all we have to do is pitch the 188 remaining seedlings into the compost pile.

Unfortunately, our capability of doing this is equal to our capability of single-handedly raising the Titanic from the ocean floor.

The usual scenario unfolds as follows: It's May 10th and we look at our puny little seedlings and decide that we really need twenty plants to fill four square feet of garden space. The seed catalog says that our plants will grow four feet tall and three feet wide. But most of us think, "Sure, they've grown that big each of the last ten years, but this year something will go wrong. They'll only grow one-third their usual size, so I better plant a lot more."

Next, we furtively look around our backyards and find homes for our sun-loving annuals behind hedges, under trees, and in other equally inhospitable places.

Now we're down to 130 seedlings, so we become missionaries, trying to convince neighbors that this annual will change their garden into a wonderland. Some neighbors humor us and take a few plants; but over the next two weeks, we ignore the fact that none of our plants has taken up residency in their gardens.

That leaves us with seventy-five seedlings.

Some get sold for 5¢ at a garden club meeting, the rest stay in six-packs for the entire summer. The leaves start to turn a sickening shade of purple or desiccate entirely. When we water our gardens, we occasionally remember to give these sad waifs a restorative drink.

Autumn approaches, and by this time we have three plants still alive, all of which would send for an ambulance if they could talk. Before winter comes, we bring these plants indoors and pot them up. Perhaps one seedling is revived and starts to grow. Finally, in January, a flower emerges from the last of the original 196 seedlings.

This plant goes on the kitchen table for everyone to see, and it's there when we open that great harbinger of eternal hope: the season's first seed catalog.

The pictures and promises are too much to resist, and our mind's eye conjures a picture of the Giverny that our backyard will become.* So, without sitting down and planning how many plants we'll need of each color and size, we order seeds — usually from companies with catalogs containing the best photographs. We ignore the fact that many of these seeds will produce plants that are inappropriate for our soil and sun exposure. And, we'll probably order enough seeds for the entire neighborhood again.

No hortiholic exists that can't identify with this lunacy. But why do we do it, over and over again?

More than anything else, I think it's our parental nature. If gardening is the eternal faith in the future, then each plant is the child that makes the future worth waiting for. Many of us would change Father Flanagan's quote "There are no bad boys," to read: "There are no bad seedlings."[†]

---

*The painter Claude Monet (1840-1926) resided in the village of Giverny, France, where he created colorful gardens that were the subjects of many of his paintings. In the world of horticulture, the name Giverny has become synonymous with Monet's home and gardens.

[†]In 1917, Father Flanagan founded Boys Town in Nebraska for "wayward boys."

I used to be as guilty of this behavior as any other gardener, but reaching middle age made me realize that I don't have the energy to coddle plants in six-packs all summer. Growing five thousand botanical children a year, when I had a mail-order business, made me into the hard-edged botanicidal gardener I am today. Now, thinning seedlings is as natural as taking a breath. So, in the case of my backyard, Darwin's Theory of Evolution is debunked every spring. There's absolutely nothing *natural* about my *selection*. It's not the strong plants that survive, but the uncrowded ones.

Spring's Offspring

To non-gardeners, it looks like a plain container of soil that redefines the word "boring." But for us, the heart races and the senses crackle with anticipation. In the beginning all is quiet, yet there's an uproar coming.

Finally, like a volcanic eruption, a great crack appears as a subterranean force moves the earth upward. Within days, a green shoot pushes above the soil and uncoils to reveal a plant: an elfin representative of the food-makers and oxygen-producers on which we all depend.

All seed-sowing gardeners feel the same excitement during germination. It's the overpowering combination of conception, childbirth, and the pride of parenthood.

Like children, these botanical offspring aren't usually conceived by plan, but by seduction. But there aren't any silk nightgowns or bursting biceps involved. Instead, the instrument of seduction is delivered to your mailbox in a plain, brown paper wrapper.

Torn open, a seed catalog spills out whose pages are filled with boisterous colors and the promise of paradise. Words such as "luminous," "pristine," "profuse," "abundant," "enticing," "graceful," and, yes, "seductive" flow from the pages and weave their spell. Before you know it, the seed dealers have their horticultural hooks into you.

For most of the year, you pride yourself on being someone with self-control, someone who keeps the padlock on the safe and doesn't overspend. But the combination of winter snow, reduced sunlight, and frozen earth sets you up for the "catalog kill." When you see the pictures of the "pristine" flowers, "abundant" vegetables, and "enticing" herbs, you go into a "luminous" funk, "gracefully" remove your wallet, and spend "profusely." Dr. Mesmer couldn't have put you into a deeper trance.

Here's how the seduction works: The first twenty pages of the catalog have dazzling pictures of new plant introductions. There are photos of blossoms so large, they hide the underlying foliage; fruits so large, they strain credulity; and prices so large, they empty your bank account. You ignore the latter and decide that you owe yourself and your garden a treat, so you circle ten of these new hybrids.

After the new introductions, the flowering plant section begins. The photographs are so sublime that they beguile you, so you circle forty or fifty annuals and perennials that you can't live without. At no time during this seduction does your mind make an effort to calculate whether your garden has enough space for even one-tenth of your selections. Likewise, you never think about the time it will take to plant the seeds and care for the seedlings.

The vegetable seed section comes next; and, while the flower pictures made you swoon, these pictures make you drool. The seed companies know that at this point in the winter you're so sick of mealy tomatoes and canned corn that these pictures are more alluring than a meal prepared by a French chef at a five-star restaurant.

The first vegetable seed section you peruse makes your sweet tooth ache, and for good reason: there's no vegetable in the world that's sweeter than fresh picked corn. So, it doesn't take too long to circle six varieties of this confectionary vegetable. Of course, it never occurs to you that you haven't ever grown more than two varieties at a time.

The next section contains a myriad of lettuce hybrids. The pictures and descriptions are so captivating that you order eight different hybrids so you can experience the ultimate salad smorgasbord. Naturally, it doesn't occur to you that, once blindfolded, even the world's greatest lettuce connoisseurs couldn't accurately name a single hybrid based solely on taste.

Eventually, you come to the tomato section. These pictures are so sensuous that the only surprise is that they haven't named any hybrids 'Better-Than-Sex,' 'Orgasmic,' or 'Forbidden Fruit.' You encircle twenty tomato varieties, or seventeen more than you've ever grown in one season.

After you've reviewed the catalog another three times, the order sheet is filled in, the numbers are added, and a check is written. The total may come to over $100, but you write the check while your brain is flat-lining.

Next comes the bittersweet anticipation of watching the mail. Your selective eye scans each day's delivery like a hawk scouring the landscape. The disappointment of today leads to even greater anticipation tomorrow. After a month, you're no different from a sleepless child on Christmas Eve.

At last the order arrives, and although you're not ready to sow a single seed, you tear open the box and run your hands over the enclosed treasures. For you, this is better than trying on all the jewelry at Tiffany's. One company, Park Seeds, plays perfectly into the metaphor by packaging their product in gold-colored packets.

Now the late winter ritual begins, and soil, flats, and fertilizers are gathered. You create such a mess that it would give Martha Stewart a heart attack. Unfortunately though, your non-gardening spouse is quite conscious and quite livid. Your promises of beauty and bounty don't reduce your partner's rage one iota. But when your significant other isn't looking, you consummate the season's first fertility rites by planting seeds.

All the expense, time, and anticipation are worth it when you see the miracle of a seedling pushing through the soil to begin its life above ground. The cycle is begun again, and you're the parent rejoicing in the life of each "childling." This event is so miraculous, so life affirming, that it rivals harvesting the first springtime salad greens, picking the first roses in May, or eating the first ripe tomato of summer.

The germination of seeds has given humanity the mythology of rebirth. Each fall the dying parent leaves behind its offspring for the next year; and, inherently, all seed-sowing gardeners feel privileged to be part of nature's unending cycle — even if we're merely a single spoke on the wheel of life.

House for Sale —
Only Bids from Gardeners Accepted

After eight years of living in a one-bedroom apartment, the imminent birth of our daughter prompted my wife and me to look for a house. Because of my interest in gardening, we sought a single home with lots of space for flower and vegetable beds. And, since I yearned for a lean-to greenhouse, I wanted the back of the house to face south with no trees that would block sunlight.

My wife's aunt and uncle were real estate salespeople, so we approached them first. When I told them about my prerequisites, they looked at me as if I were in the market for a missile silo. They had expertise in distance from schools and markets, in-ground swimming pools, enclosed porches, and two-car garages. Their years of experience in no way prepared them for the priorities of a committed gardener.

Whenever they called for an appointment to see a home, they were never able to get information about the direction the backyard faced or if it was filled with trees. We'd invariably find that the home was completely inappropriate for gardening. Eventually, I had to compromise; we settled for a home that needed three huge trees removed to have enough sunlight for a vegetable garden.

The episode made me realize that the real estate industry should offer a different method for gardeners to select a home. To portray each property, a more horticulturally-attuned guide would be needed, whether it's a multiple listing book, a video, or an Internet web site.

Any of these sources should contain the following:

- Photograph or video: Dispense with any depiction of the house, since it's of secondary importance. Instead, several garden pictures would be included along with a property survey.

The latter would not only show lot dimensions, compass orientation, and acreage, but also the location of all trees and shrubs.

- Local Ordinances: Since non-gardeners govern many municipalities, there may be ordinances that thwart gardeners. So, we'd need the following information:

  > Compost pile regulations- Yes, there really are towns that have laws against compost piles. For some reason, many elected officials think it's better to take your grass clippings to a dump than it is to recycle them into the soil to create a beautiful garden.

  > Fences- Laws concerning backyard as well as front yard fences should be listed. Many municipalities think it's OK for your next-door neighbors to create a basketball court on your street, but not for you to erect a fence to protect your front yard garden from street athletes.

  > Easements- Do most cable companies have the right to place their cable in your garden to hook-up your neighbors? You bet they do! And, even though other utilities have to put their materials at least eighteen inches underground in states like New Jersey, the cable companies put their wire barely below the surface. It's at just the right depth for your rototiller to rip it to shreds. But although this may be an outlet for your anger, your catharsis will be short-lived, since the cable company will know immediately that you're the culprit who's disrupted service. And, since your neighbors consider watching TV more important than your ability to garden, they'll despise you as much as the cable companies do.

- Location: Exclude information about distance from schools, malls, and trains; include distance from public mulch distribution sites and travel time to garden clubs, major flower shows, and public gardens.

- Population Distribution: I'm not talking about religious or racial profiling; I'm referring to information on the average number of garden club members per square mile. Aside from horticultural camaraderie, it's especially important to have allies when your neighbors join en-masse to try to change the zoning laws just because you use fresh cow manure in your compost pile.

- Soil Analysis: This would include macronutrients and micronutrients, as well as a breakdown of percent clay, sand, and loam. With this information, you'll know in advance that a home site has impermeable soil that would be ideal for growing rice, and little else.

- Oven: The most highly prized oven would be the trusty gas oven whose pilot is always on. The temperature inside an oven with a constant pilot is about 85°F, which is perfect for seed germination.

- Windows: This would include the size of each window, the direction it faces, and the number of hours that sunlight passes through it per day during all four seasons.

- Home Microclimates: This would include a full description of growing areas in and around the house, showing yearly temperature and humidity ranges. These parameters would be reported for all living spaces as well as for the attic, crawl space, garage, front and back patios, and shed.

- Financing: Although information about an assumable mortgage is occasionally helpful, it is secondary in importance to assumable bulbs, perennials, shrubs, trees, and other incidentals like greenhouses, cold frames, garden ornaments, and tools. It should be stated which plants and accessories are negotiable and which ones the sellers will take with them.

Feel free to give this list to your real estate agents. I'm sure they'll appreciate information about your special requirements. But since my home already gets more than its share of sabotage on Mischief Night, please don't tell them whom they can thank for this innocent little wish list.

Happy ~~house~~ garden hunting!

A Plea to Steven Spielberg

All right, Mr. Spielberg, I admit it.

I'm a librarian, and librarians are supposed to be enthralled and consumed by English literature, but I'm not. In the old days, library schools laughed at anyone who got within sniffing distance of their campuses who wasn't an English major. Well, times have changed, and that's why a biology major like me was eventually inflicted upon the patrons of the Camden County Library in New Jersey.

Oh, I like English literature all right. As a matter of fact, I think Charles Dickens is the greatest novelist of all time. I swear that when I first read *A Tale of Two Cities*, I could actually smell the blood in the streets of revolutionary Paris.

Having said this, it's time to be honest. I happen to be a very visual person, and, aside from gardens, there's no art form that moves me more than movies. If they're good, I'm enraptured.

But that "if" is a very big "if." The "if's" I'm talking about are
- if the actors are believable,
- if the screenplay is genuine and I actually believe that people would say those lines, and
- if the locations are believable.

Provided that directors like you give me those three things, I feel like I'm sucked into the picture and become part of the action. I'm so transported that my wife and daughter are usually embarrassed by my behavior at the cinema. Nobody in the theater laughed louder during *When Harry Met Sally*, screamed louder during *Alien*, or got angrier during *One Flew Over the Cuckoo's Nest*.

Unfortunately, my "if" list can get very much in the way of my enjoyment. If any one of the three doesn't work, I get itchy. If two don't work, I start looking at my watch. If all three don't work, I leave and find a better way to spend two hours of my limited life.

When I was younger, location was at the bottom of my "if" list, but once I became an ardent gardener, it went to the top. Suddenly, movies that I would have otherwise considered marvelous are marked down a notch.

Here are just a few examples:

— Dr. Zhivago

This sweeping love story, played against the backdrop of the Russian Revolution, earned five Academy Awards. It enthralled me when I was a teenager. Then, after becoming an avid gardener, I saw it again in video. For a while, I was again pulled into the movie; but during Dr. Zhivago's first spring in Siberia, wild daffodils were shown blooming everywhere.

Suddenly, the magic was gone, and I was zapped out of the movie and back into my living room. I thought the only place that those types of Narcissi bloomed in profusion was in and around Spain.

Sure enough, when I watched the credits at the end, there it was in living color: "Filmed In Spain."

— Enchanted April

This rollicking comedy, about four English women who escape from dreary London to find love in Portofino, was a big hit. It really was a laugh-a-minute, and came very close to reeling me in. The only problem was that all the flowering plants in the movie actually bloom during the summer in Italy. Did the director of this movie really think that it would have been less comedic if it were named *Enchanted July*?

— Wolf

This movie, which mixed horror and romance and starred Jack Nicholson and Michelle Pfeifer, was mostly mesmerizing. But unfortunately, whoever wrote the screenplay had a sketchy idea of the progression of seasons. In the opening scenes, Nicholson is in his car on a wintertime business trip to Vermont. Ice and snow are everywhere. Suddenly, a wolf runs out of the woods and Nicholson slams on the brakes. His car skids on the ice and hits the wolf, but it eventually bites him and changes him into a werewolf.

The next week, Nicholson is in New York City's Central Park, where the dark green foliage on the trees reveals that it's mid-summer. Now I know that Vermont is north of New York City, but it's not that far north. And they do have a summer growing season in Vermont.

As much as anyone else, I believe in poetic license, but with this flick, the screenwriter's license should be revoked!

— In the Line of Fire

In this thriller, Clint Eastwood tries to protect a U.S. president from assassination during a fall re-election campaign. Almost every scene filled the theater with palpable tension, but one left me shaking my head. The producers spent megabucks on locations and actors, then wasted their money by showing three dollars worth of tulips in a vase. I have to tell you: I've seen a lot of cut tulips, but I can't remember ever seeing them in bloom before November ... and I'll bet you can't either.

— Mr. Holland's Opus

As you already know, there's someone on the set of each movie called "continuity." Since you can shoot the same scene over days, weeks, or even months, continuity's job is to make sure that hair, glasses, clothes, and other incidentals are identical for the same scene.

Well, in this film, about a music teacher's career, Mr. or Ms. Continuity dropped the botanical ball.

In the scene in which Mr. Holland, played by Richard Dreyfus, hears that John Lennon died, he's in a classroom whose windows show deciduous trees in full-leaf. Later that day, he arrives at home where there's snow on the ground. But when he gets into the house, the view from the window again shows trees in full-leaf. So, in the course of one day, we go from summer to winter to summer. It was enough to make a gardener wonder if this movie was about a music teacher or time travel.

— Amistad

This historical epic, which you directed, Mr. Spielberg, was one of the most important movies of 1997. There was something for everyone to learn, as people of all races came face-to-face with the terrors of slavery. Some historians have nit-picked about a few of the details, but still agree that the film is fundamentally accurate. On the other hand, this movie would drive a botanist batty.

In one moving scene, Cinque walks with John Quincy Adams into the former president's sunroom. As Adams shows off his plants, one specimen captures the West African's attention: an African violet. Flute, violin, and harp music supply the emotive audio as Cinque recalls the plant and lowers his nose to smell the flowers. While he's sniffing, Adams tells him, "I can't tell you how difficult that was to come by." Cinque's recognition of the plant helps graft a botanical bond between him and Adams, and for most moviegoers it was a special moment. But for me, it was the weakest point in an otherwise exceptional movie.

Here's the scoop: African violets first came to the attention of Western Civilization in 1892, when they were discovered by Baron von Saint Paul in the plant's native area of East Africa, not West Africa. So, Cinque never would have laid eyes on the diminutive plant. Second, African violets didn't arrive in this country until 1894, or forty-six years after John Quincy Adams died. And third, although hybridizers have bred almost every leaf shape and flower color into African violets, they've never been able to add scent to the blossoms.

So although this movie gave us an indelible picture of the brutal realities of the slave trade, it also left me wondering if the document-ed history of the African violet is wrong. Here's my take on what the screenwriter must have believed when he wrote this scene: John Quincy Adams went incognito to East Africa to unearth an African violet (hence the reason why the plant "was so difficult to come by"). Then, when he returned, he must have sprayed the plant with his aftershave lotion — something that gave the plant a scent, but which ultimately caused its demise. If true, these conjectures would mean that fifty-four years later, an African violet made its way to this continent for the sec-ond time.

So, for this scene, either the screenwriter is one hell of a great a horticultural historian or one hell of a lousy one. Which choice do you think I would make?

— *Primary Colors*

This wonderful film, about a "fictional" southern Democratic governor who runs for the presidency, was a thinly veiled depiction of a Bill Clinton campaign. It had outstanding performances from John Travolta, who was a perfect caricature of Clinton; Emma Thompson, who managed to drop her English accent to transform herself into the "Hillary Clinton" role; and Cathy Bates, in an Oscar-nominated role as the tough-as-nails, heart-of-gold character.

And, the movie itself was golden, except for two critical scenes.

The first was a Thanksgiving barbecue at the southern governor's house. As we all know, Thanksgiving occurs anytime from November 22nd to 28th. By that time, even in the Southeastern United States, deciduous leaves are either on the ground or are hanging from trees in blowsy shades of yellow, orange, or red.

But at this barbecue, the deciduous trees had leaves that were the deep green of summer. Someone must have realized that the environment had to look more like November, so dried leaves were placed equidistant from each other around the set. Regrettably, all this did was make the green trees stand out even more.

The following February, after the New Hampshire primary, the action again switches to the South, and once more all the trees appear dark green.

My only question is, didn't the director of photography ever look at the background of these scenes? Some damn good professional photographers taught me that the background is extremely important in any type of photography. On the other hand, it's possible that they didn't know what they were talking about and background really doesn't matter at all.

And, if you believe that, I'd like to sell you the lost continent of Atlantis for a mere $50 million.

****

The problem with these and many other movies is that directors are too busy directing to become gardeners. But in all fairness, no one can expect you to take time off from creating your works of art to become plant nuts.

Fortunately, the problem is easily solved.

Look, you pay big bucks to outside consultants like doctors for medical dramas, lawyers for courtroom dramas, cowboys for westerns, and engineers for techno-thrillers. Obviously, what you need is a biologist/gardener for any movie that contains a member of the plant kingdom. Since that means virtually every film, there should be a full-time gardener slot at every studio.

I guess what I'm really saying, Mr. Spielberg, is that I'm your man. I already get swallowed up by movies and truly care about your final product. So, you might as well hire someone who wants to protect the movie experience for his fellow gardeners.

And, if you hire me, I'll be able to realize one of my great fantasies. It'll go something like this: I'm at the library and I get asked a real stumper of an English literature reference question; something like, "Please explain the allegorical meaning of Samuel Coleridge's *The Rime of the Ancient Mariner.*"

I'll be able to whip out my sunglasses and say, "Sorry, I'm needed on location in California by Columbia Pictures. They're not sure if some giant redwoods have to be removed for a scene of Jack Nicholson supposedly playing a lumberjack in Australia.

"Hasta la vista baby."

Mothballs on Flower Stems

A librarian I know was a budding gardener who, one year, decided to force her first pot of bulbs in the library she managed.

Unfortunately, she picked paperwhites.*

When the first florets opened and their powerful scent wafted throughout the library, she contacted me and asked, "Does this smell of burnt rubber get any better as more flowers open?"

I chuckled, then told her she could expect the scent to increase geometrically as the number of open flowers doubles, and then doubles again. Luckily, someone on her staff liked the odor, so the paperwhites were quickly expunged from the premises and the librarian's first bulb-forcing efforts ended abruptly.

So why are paperwhites one of the most common bulbs sold at local garden centers and supermarkets every fall? The answer is that there are many of us who adore them. In effect, this one bulb has split the horticultural world down the middle. I think that in the entire history of gardening, there's never been a gardener undecided about paperwhites. They're either abhorred or loved, nothing in between.

Over the years, I've heard both positive and negative comments about them. On the positive side, the adjectives have been standard, but on the negative side, they've been outrageous.

One was related by garden writer Melissa Sinclair Stevens, whose son smelled her paperwhites and asked, "Mom, do you smell airplane glue or something?"†

Other gardeners have noted that paperwhites made them nauseated or likened their odor to used pet litter or even soiled diapers.

One year, I talked a neighbor into buying a bulb-forcing collection.

---

*Paperwhites are daffodils native to the Mediterranean region and are classified as tazetta narcissi.

† From the Zanthan Gardens website:

http://www.zanthan.com/gardens/gardenlog/index.html

He enjoyed forcing the crocuses and tulips into bloom, but then came paperwhites. The morning after the first flowers opened, I noticed the pot outside his front door. Later that day, his wife gave me a look of scorn and asked me why stench-ridden bulbs were included in the collection. When I told her that I enjoyed the scent, she looked at me as if I were from Neptune. To this day, I think she's convinced that anyone who likes the smell of paperwhites needs to wear a tight-fitting jacket in a padded room.

My wife, Arlene, is definitely among those who hope for the eventual extinction of this bulb. For eleven months of the year, she enjoys looking at the flowering plants behind the sliding glass door of our greenhouse. But when paperwhites are in bloom, she wants the door locked tight. I've no doubt that she's considered hiring a bulb-napper more than once for these olfactory offenders.

So what is it that makes their scent so powerfully pervasive?

Several perfumers think the scent of Narcissus is similar to naphthalene, a chemical popularly known as mothballs.* And, come to think of it, if one looks at them from across the room, they do look like clusters of mothballs sitting on flower stems.†

Fortunately, there's hope in sight. Bulb hybridizers have been busy trying to tone down the scent of paperwhites and are making progress. They went in the wrong direction with 'Ziva,' which I can smell through the walls of my greenhouse, but 'Nazareth' and 'Grand Primo' have gentler aromas. So there are alternatives, even for gardeners with more delicate nostrils.

As for me, when the first killing frost turns all my garden flowers black, I know I won't be able to stop myself from buying another batch of powerful paperwhites.

There's just one thing that confuses me: When the flowers are dead and the pot is ready for the trash heap, do you suppose I have to add hazardous waste stickers, or are pet litter/diaper-scented flowers exempt from such a warning?

---

*Tovah Martin, *The Essence of Paradise: Fragrant Plants for Indoor Gardens* (Boston: Little Brown and Company, 1991), 18.

†In fact, the allusion to mothballs is not farfetched: Naphthalene-related compounds have been shown to contribute to flower scent in several plants. In addition, the other mothball chemical, paradichlorobenzene, is related to another class of flower scent chemicals: benzenoids.

"Of course he doesn't know about it...
he thinks I like that steaming eco-crazed
mountain of garbage."

6

GARDENERS AND
NON-GARDENERS

Bridging the Gap

A FRIEND OF MINE WAS ONCE IN charge of creating a flower garden at a nature center. He made an excellent start by planting scads of annuals and perennials; but unfortunately, the director of the center was a non-gardener. So, when my friend spread cow manure in the fall to improve the soil, the sensitive-nosed director cancelled all future plans for the garden.

The episode made me realize that gardeners and non-gardeners look at their worlds through such different eyes, they might best exist on separate galaxies. However, they not only live on the same planet, but are often next-door neighbors.

So, since we have to live together, I think gardeners and non-gardeners should take a lesson from our diplomats who serve in foreign countries. Their first order of business is always to learn the language of the natives. Although I know that most Americans speak English and that we should be able to communicate with one another, I also know that gardeners and non-gardeners are so different that it often takes a translator for them to understand one another.

I thought I'd take a step in the right direction by providing a translation guide that will help bridge the gap between these two human sub-species. So, whether you're a gardener or not, I think you'll benefit from my thirty years of code-breaking experience.

Gardener: "Do you garden at all?"
Non-gardener: "Oh yeah, several times a year."
Translation: "Oh yeah, I pay the neighborhood kid to mow my lawn, and several times a year I look out the window and watch him work."

Non-gardener: "How much time do you spend gardening during the week?"

Gardener: "A couple of hours."

Translation: "On weekends during the growing season, I'm in the garden from sun-up to sundown. The rest of the year I spend my waking hours coddling my indoor plants and obsessing on what next year's garden will look like."

Gardener: "Have you ever grown your own vegetables?"

Non-gardener: "Yeah, the Mrs. and I used to do that a lot, but now that the kids are grown and out of the house, we've stopped."

Translation: "One time our kids whined until we agreed to take them to one of those 'pick-your-own' farms. We picked strawberries, got full of mud, and threw out our backs. The next time the kids asked to go, we turned up the volume on the television to drown them out."

Gardener: "What do you think about gardeners?"

Non-gardener: "Everybody has a right to pursue their own hobby. After all, you guys do beautify the neighborhood."

Translation: "I think you should all be committed. Anyone who can spend all day outside in the blazing sun, staring at flowers and slinging manure, needs five electroshock therapy treatments a week."

Non-gardener: "What do you think about non-gardeners?"

Gardener: "Everybody has a right to their own interests. After all, you do appreciate how gardeners beautify the neighborhood."

Translation: "I think you should all be committed. Anyone who doesn't understand the joy of spending a sunny summer day in the garden, standing in fertile soil, coddling flowers and vegetables, and spreading compost needs five electroshock therapy treatments a week."

Gardener: "It's taken weeks, but my husband and I finally finished the front yard rock garden. Did I mention that we not only took the plants from our last home, but also had the rocks moved? We had to pay an extra $3,000, but I just couldn't leave them at the property we sold."

Non-gardener: "No, I didn't know that about the rocks, but I can see why you moved them. I've never seen a rock garden like yours."

Translation: "Actually, your front yard looks like a dump. Are you sure you didn't drop one of those rocks on your head before you moved?"

Gardener: "How's that bonsai doing that I gave you last Christmas?"

Non-gardener: "Oh, great. I admire it every day!"

Translation: "I threw it in the trash a month ago. Whatever possessed you to give me such an idiotic gift when you know that I can't even keep a cactus alive for more than a week?"

Non-gardener: "I had multicolored caterpillars climbing on a few weeds in my backyard, so I had to use an herbicide on the weeds and insecticide on the bugs."

Gardener: "Good for you! I know you want to have a weed- and insect-free lawn, so you did the right thing."

Translation: "Didn't you know that those were monarch butterfly worms feeding on milkweed — their main source of food? I've gotten one hundred local gardeners to sign a petition complaining about your asinine behavior. I'm sending copies to the EPA, Greenpeace, as well as to horticultural and environmental magazines. You can expect picketers and a crew from *60 Minutes* to show up any day now to make your life a misery."

Gardener: "I hope you don't mind the compost pile that's next to my fence."

Non-gardener: "No, that's fine; I know that compost is good for plants."

Translation: "So far, I have seventy-five signatures on my petition to force you to get rid of your foul-smelling haven for rats. I'll get twenty-five more, then send copies to the township committee, the police chief, and newspapers. I hope you have to pay a hefty fine and that your name and address are splashed all over the media."

Non-gardener: "I cut the grass in your front yard."

Gardener: "What a nice thing to do. I really appreciate it!"

Translation, Non-gardener: "Because of your lack of common decency, you let weeds grow in your lawn. Lately, I've noticed that one of them showed up in my front yard, so you forced me to take care of your grass. Yesterday, I not only cut your grass, but spread expensive weed killer on it. I wish you'd just move away, so I'd have neighbors who are considerate of others."

Translation, Gardener: "You had the unmitigated gall not only to cut my grass, but to put herbicide on it? Don't you know I'm an organic gardener? The "weed" you're talking about is clover that I planted on purpose — because it fixes nitrogen in the soil and feeds grass without using chemicals. Now you've wiped it out and poisoned my front yard with an herbicide. I'll probably have to wait at least a year before I can sow more clover seed. In addition, some of your herbicide wound up in my flowerbeds and killed plants that I started from seed years ago.

If I ever so much as see you set foot in my front yard again, I'll call the police and have you cited for trespassing. I wish you'd just move away, so I'd have neighbors who respect people's property."

****

In conclusion, although gardeners and non-gardeners will never understand why people in the other group act the way they do, I'm hoping that this first attempt at a translation guide may make communication possible — however slim the odds.

The Non-Gardeners Among Us

They're everywhere: in our homes and neighborhoods, and among our families, co-workers, and friends. These are the people for whom the word "garden" will always be a noun and never a verb. It wouldn't be accurate to say that they live in a separate, parallel universe. Actually, they live in a separate, perpendicular universe.*

We know who they are, and they certainly know who we are. Once a person reaches adulthood, the pattern is set: either you get a thrill by coaxing a plant to horticultural glory or you don't.

While we don't understand their disinterest, we have to admit that gardening is very work-intensive. There are a lot of hobbies that don't burn nearly as many calories, but we think the ends justify the means, non-gardeners don't.

In most of the United States, gardeners and non-gardeners are easily distinguished by observing their lawn-care activities. Non-gardeners see the lawn as an end in itself, and the definitive source of pride. Their quest is to produce a lawn that would make a golf course superintendent drool. To the contrary, gardeners view the lawn as a canvas onto which they paint picturesque landscapes. The lawn isn't the finished product, but a beginning. We turn under large swaths of lawn to begin our works of art. Non-gardeners stand agape at our destructiveness and think to themselves, "It takes all kinds."

Everyone's heard the saying that one person's heaven is another's hell. That's certainly the case with gardeners and non-gardeners. This became obvious to me when my daughter, Beth, and her friend Sara helped me plant annuals in our front yard. Pieces of lawn disappeared

---

*Non-gardening physicists who think that perpendicular universes don't exist need only spend one afternoon with me at the Philadelphia Flower Show. After three hours, they'll either believe I inhabit a separate, perpendicular universe or want to send me to one.

to prepare for a new flowerbed. Sara, who lived in a condominium, said they would never be permitted to do this.

I stared at her, uncomprehendingly.

I'm sure that to many of the condo's residents this "hands off" policy is heaven-on-earth. To me it would be a living hell. I view my land with hope, because of the potential beauty and harvest it can provide — similar to the reverential view Pearl Buck described in *The Good Earth*. To the contrary, non-gardening condo residents would be delighted to call their yard "Somebody Else's Good Earth."

Admittedly, during some summer days it can be oppressively hot, but never too hot to visit a famous garden. I can remember one trip my family made to Longwood Gardens when it was a humid 96°F. After enduring ten minutes in the blast furnace, my wife said, "I can't believe I'm here!" Through my own rose-colored glasses, I replied, "Yeah, isn't it *great*?"

My mother was the first person who made me aware of the peculiar views of non-gardeners. When my wife and I began our married life, we lived in an apartment, so I convinced my parents to let me use their backyard for a vegetable garden. I obtained large tree branches to support my tomato plants, used composted leaves for mulch, and removed some of their lawn to create a carrot patch.

It was not my mother's idea of a beautiful backyard.

After one look, she threatened to move to an apartment rather than view the vegetable garden. I retorted, "OK, but make sure you get a place with large windows that face south, so I can use your sills for my seedlings."

My wife, Arlene, is a rare individual who occasionally has one foot in both camps. After living with an avid gardener for over thirty years, she's absorbed enough information to occasionally amaze beginning gardeners. Her favorite story that she relates to my gardening friends is how she beat me out of a blue ribbon at the Philadelphia Flower Show. Nevertheless, I suspect that if I suddenly keeled over, my garden would be overlaid with concrete before my body got cold.

Much like the non-artist who visits a museum, non-gardeners can enjoy a garden display, but they aren't inspired to create. They may appreciate the beauty and bounty we provide, but they're immune to the gravitational pull of our obsession.

We garden nuts catch the disease and keep it forever.

Non-Gardening "Gardeners"

I think that even if I had a PhD in horticulture, there would always be areas of gardening that confound me.

Aside from the gardeners I've already described, there's also a group of people who populate garden clubs and win flower show awards, but who don't garden. They have their "ghost growers" take care of plants all year, then enter the plants in flower shows under their (i.e., not the real grower's) name.*

I have to admit that I just don't get it.

This business reminds me of when I took up golf as a teenager and lied about my score on one hole. The adult scorekeeper looked through my eyes and straight into my soul; then he said, "Art, you aren't fooling anyone except yourself." That man changed my life forever. I had given a lower score because I wanted respect. He made me realize that respect is only earned through hard work and self-accomplishment.

This brings me to the topic of "non-gardening 'gardeners,'" and begs the question: What are they trying to prove? Although I've never been rich enough to pay someone to grow entries for me to exhibit at a flower show, I can venture the following guesses about the motivation of non-gardening "gardeners":

1. "I can hire a better gardener and buy better plants than you."

This reason is not as implausible as it sounds. I've seen this type of behavior in action. But why go to all the bother? Why not have neutral accountants compare the total net worth of the two non-gardening "gardeners" and have done with it?

---

*In this section, I'm not referring to gardeners who oversee the maintenance of plants on a massive scale. It would be impossible for them to do so without the aid of a greenhouse staff.

2. "I believe that I deserve to win these awards, even though I didn't have anything to do with growing the plants exhibited in my name."

My first question is, are these people permanent residents of Disney's Fantasyland? Their logic relates to number one, but in this case, the non-gardening "gardeners" somehow think the hired gardeners hands are actually their hands. If non-gardening "gardeners" believe they deserve the awards, they need to pay a visit to their dictionaries and look up the meaning of "deserve." In my copy of *The Oxford English Dictionary*, I couldn't find anything vaguely related to "buying your way to fame."

This behavior exists in many other endeavors, the most glaring being ownership of sports teams. There are some owners who practically sabotage their teams' efforts by undermining the managers they hire. Then, when their teams win championships, they steal the limelight from those most responsible for the victories. The obvious question is, do the owners really go to their graves thinking they had more to do with the championships than supplying money?

This subject begets a few more questions: If non-gardening "gardeners" really believe that the work of others equals "their work," where does the chicanery end? I consider gardens and container plants to be art forms. So, if non-gardening "gardeners" think they're truly deserving, do they also buy paintings and scratch out the real painter's name and substitute theirs? If they don't, why don't they? I can't understand why they'd claim that one purchased art form is their creation, but not another.

3. "I know I didn't grow these plants and my name doesn't really deserve to be on a trophy, but my plants help make a flower show successful, which in turn supports a wonderful horticultural organization."

I have no argument with this logic. Although I've mellowed about this type of non-gardening "gardener," many of my fellow flower show exhibitors remain steadfast in their disdain. I understand their feelings — especially when blue ribbons are at stake — but I think it's time for them to take the broader view. If the rules allow a philanthropist to do this at flower shows, that's fine. The bottom line is that visitors to major flower shows would "oooh" and "aaaaah" a lot less without this type of non-gardening "gardener."

My wife once complained about them, and said that if she were in charge of a flower show, she wouldn't allow these exhibitors to put plants in her show. I responded that her press releases would brag that her shows have the widest aisles of any flower show in the United States.

In short, when it comes to flower shows and non-gardening "gardeners," we may love them or leave them, but we'll always need them, so mums the word.

The Eyes Have It

Two people go to an ophthalmologist, look at a chart, tell the doctor the right letters, and are told they have 20/20 vision. This isn't out of the ordinary, except that letters are the only things that these patients are likely to agree upon.

One is a gardener, the other anything but.

They agree on L, Z, V, H, Q, and B, but most definitely disagree on G, A, R, D, E, and N. The same light goes through their pupils, but each brain has a different take on the photons and what they mean. When it comes to G-A-R-D-E-N, one sees an ash tree, perennials, and shrubs; the other sees shrubs and a perennial pain in the ... well, you get the idea.

Over many decades, I've had the disadvantage of hearing non-gardeners tell me what they think they see. This has permitted me to collect enough information to create a chart that documents their misperceptions.

It's included here purely for entertainment, but it has an additional use: I've decided to send a copy to my eye doctor, who just happens to be a gardener. I'm hoping that it ultimately replaces letter charts, so physicians will be able to more accurately diagnose visual disorders.

But as for a cure? That would take one incredible pair of glasses.

****

Objects or events	Non-gardener perception or response	Gardener perception or response
Compost	Vermin, filth, bubonic plague	Powerful potion
Falling leaves	A wasted weekend	Fodder for compost
Rabbit	Peter Rabbit	Peter Raptor
Chipmunk	Alvin, Chip & Dale	Underground metropolis
Squirrel	Fluffy tail, fun to feed	Contortionist that destroys birdfeeders while twisted into the shape of a pretzel
Wild violets in the lawn	"Horrors! Grab the weed killer."	"Hooray! Grab the camera."
5" tall front yard grass	Shame, stay indoors, pull down the shades	Healthy, green grass at the perfect height
Two cubic yards of clean, composted cow manure	Twenty cubic yards of freshly dropped cow manure	Two cubic yards that guarantee a great garden
Hanging plants	Décor	Hanging cuttings, waiting to be plucked
Car	Status symbol	Something used to haul plants and mulch
Plastic plant	Plant	Oxymoron

Objects or events	Non-gardener perception or response	Gardener perception or response
Someone planting a rhododendron in full sun	Someone planting a plant	Someone inflicting cruel and unusual punishment
Someone wiring a bonsai	Someone inflicting cruel and unusual punishment	A master artisan helping a plant reach perfection
A visit to the desert outside of Las Vegas	"Get me out of here!"	"I never knew the desert could be so beautiful."
A visit to a Las Vegas casino	"I never knew a town could be so exciting."	"Get me out of here!"
A visit to Redwood National Park	"I'm wet, cold, and 300 miles from San Francisco."	"Who would've thought that heaven was only 300 miles from San Francisco?"
An old-fashioned garden center	"Where are the gas grills?"	"What's the spending limit on my credit card?"
Plastic bags filled with leaves	Bags of garbage	Free bags of mulch for next year's garden
People buying canned corn in the summer	People buying corn	People who've forgotten to take their medication
People wearing Wellie boots	People who've forgotten to take their medication	Potential life-long companions

"Wow...what a gorgeous weed!"

7

ABERRANT BEHAVIOR
IN GARDENERS

Where Weed Is Never a Weed

LET ME CLEAR THE AIR, SO TO SPEAK, from the outset: I've "never inhaled" (to quote President Clinton), nor have I sought nor bought the stuff. As a child and young adult, I suffered from asthma and still have occasional wheezes. So smoking anything, except perhaps salmon or ham, would necessitate a quick trip to an emergency room.

Still, as a gardener I'm intrigued by Mary Jane, and her sisters Grass, Reefer, Pot, Roaches, Weed, and Marijuana. Forget about the fact that it's a controlled substance, and that anyone who grows it can wind up in a rent-free apartment known as prison. I've taken a hard look at the plant (meaning that like President Carter, I've sinned "in my heart many times") and I think it's gorgeous.

It has graceful palmate leaves that wave at you enticingly, and it grows upright, so it would add a charming vertical background in any garden. Best of all, it stays where it's planted and doesn't use botanical blitzkrieg to overtake your backyard.

So — using gun lobby logic — just because other people misuse the plant, why should I, as an avid gardener, be forbidden to grow it? The obvious answer is that, like the handgun, there are too many people misusing it. And they not only misuse it, they blatantly misuse it.

And, in some cases, blatantly grow it to misuse it.

But let me explain.

Back in the 1980s I worked in downtown Philadelphia. Some people hate the crowds, but I've always found what we call Center City, to be a lovely, very alive place. In addition, Philadelphians are lucky because they have several squares that are small green oases to which downtown workers and residents can escape.

My favorite retreat has always been Rittenhouse Square, a resplendent spot containing fountains, sculpture, trees, azaleas, and an expansive lawn. I was lucky that it lay on a direct route to and from my job, so I used to walk through it twice a day. I may have been on my way to, or coming back from, a hard day's labor, but the Square always soothed my soul.

What I especially relished were the myriad of plants that became signposts of the changing seasons. Like most people, I particularly enjoyed spring — the trees became clouds of soft green foliage, a carpet of grass hid the cold mud of winter, and creamy azalea blossoms floated above the walkways.

On one spring morning I changed my route, venturing onto the grass to get a full view of the azaleas. And it was on the grass that I saw Grass.

Tucked slightly under an azalea was a 15" Marijuana plant ... in broad daylight ... in the center of Rittenhouse Square ... in the center of Philadelphia. The chances of a bird carrying a Marijuana seed in its gut, depositing it here, and the plant growing without any human assistance were probably equal to a bird's chances of flying safely through a black hole.

Meaning the Weed wasn't a weed.

So somebody had planted Mary Jane in a place where they thought no one would notice her. But he or she didn't figure on a snooping gardener.

I didn't know what to do at first, but then thought it would be fun to point it out to the park guard usually in attendance. However, it was 7:30AM and neither he nor anyone else was in the square, so I decided to show it to him after work.

That afternoon I returned to Rittenhouse Square, saw the guard, went to find the Divine Miss "M," but she was gone!

In spite of the fact that no one else was in Rittenhouse Square that morning, whoever had been growing the Marijuana must have seen me looking at it. Not wanting to risk the loss of the unpotted Pot, the grower removed it, thus ending my fleeting first relationship with Mary Jane.

Two years later, I was living in New Jersey, less than ten miles from Philadelphia. One neighbor, Eddie, wanted to learn how to grow vegetables from seeds, and asked me to teach him how to go about it.

He learned quickly, and by late June had a thriving vegetable patch along the side of his house.

Then, one weekday afternoon, I had off from work and went down the street to check on his garden. There were rows of robust plants that made me feel proud that I had taught him so well: First there were tomatoes, then collard greens, Marijuana, lettuce, onions, and ... whoa!

My eyes retraced their passage over Eddie's vegetable bed and widened when I saw the thriving row of 12" Marijuana plants. My brain hiccupped and didn't accept the visual input for a few seconds, but eventually processed the information. Sure enough, Mary Jane was outdoors prancing in the raw for everyone to see.

I started laughing and couldn't stop — my first foray into teaching someone how to garden had resulted in a neat row of Pot in the middle of a vegetable garden.

After a minute, I figured out how I'd confront Eddie.

That evening, I telephoned him and avoided the subject at hand for a few minutes; then I steered the conversation toward Mary Jane.

"Eddie, I'm really proud of how marvelous your vegetable garden looks."

"Thanks," he said enthusiastically.

"Yeah, you're going to have some wonderful produce for your wife and kids this summer."

I paused then said, "Well, anyway, I had a look at your garden this afternoon, and everything looked very healthy. But I noticed a bunch of weeds next to your collard greens, so I got rid of them for you."

I decided to let the smoke slowly settle, thus beginning the longest ten seconds of my life.

One ...
Two ...
Three ...
Four ...
Five ...
Six ...
Seven ...
Eight ...
Nine ...
Ten ...

It was torture for me to wait this long, but I'm sure it was worse for Eddie.

Finally, I broke the tension by saying, "It's alright, Eddie, I didn't touch your Marijuana."

"Oh, OK, yeah, well, thanks, I've, uh, got to go now," he murmured, then hung up.

I had a feeling that he might head for the medicine cabinet to grab a tranquilizer, but realized it was more likely that he would set off in another direction.

The next day, I passed by Eddie's garden again, and, lo and behold, one of the rows in his vegetable patch was gone — the one between the collard greens and lettuce.

So, unwittingly, I was again responsible for the unearthing, so to speak, of a bewitching but illegal plant. Unlike the Feds, I didn't have to carry a nightstick, tap a phone, break down a door, fly a helicopter, or use a semi-automatic weapon.

It seems that all I have to do is look at Marijuana and it disappears into thick air.

Given this talent, I think that eventually I'll be named the U.S. Drug Czar. There's just one problem: Every time the comely Miss Mary Jane is confiscated, I know I'll leave my office to leer at her.

I admit it: We botanical voyeurs just can't kick the habit.

Treats from the Trash

I've already mentioned in the Digger's Dictionary that gardeners can be divided into various groups depending on their level of experience, and by experience I'm referring to the number of plants they've killed (see page 20).

But there's also another way to segregate gardeners, based on the disdain they're willing to accept from their neighbors for the sake of their hobby. Probably more than 98% of today's gardeners care more about their relationship with their neighbors than their relationship with their plants. They are able to conform to society's norms and manage to keep their hobby from taking over their life. These gardeners may get upset about a plant dying in their garden, but aren't willing to risk humiliation by sinking to aberrant behavior to save it. They spend their lives in relative harmony with their family, neighbors, and garden.

Then there are gardeners like me, who put our relationships with plants ahead of our relationships with our neighbors. We may feel humiliation because of our non-conformity, but it changes nothing — our plants come first.

Although I've recently toned down my fervency for blue ribbons — meaning I'm not willing to shorten my life span in return for flower show awards — there's still one activity that especially embarrasses my friends and family. As you may have guessed from the title of this section, the activity to which I refer is trash picking.

I was probably labeled an eccentric when I turned under my first shovelful of front yard turf to create a flowerbed. But I completely lost any respect my neighbors still had for me when I began scrounging in their trash for garden-related harvests.

Some items that I've recycled into my garden include a patio table and chairs that needed a bit of paint, old windows that I used for a cold frame, and small boulders that became part of my first rock garden.

Aside from the above items, the most common things I take from my neighbors' trash are tree leaves and grass clippings. The average organic gardener would think that my neighbors are nuts for throwing out free mulch. On the other hand, I revel in their spendthrift behavior. My yearly cycle follows theirs in the same way that a predator follows its prey.

Here's how a typical year unfolds:

Spring and Summer

On the first warm weekend in spring my neighbors descend upon the local garden center, where they buy expensive lawn fertilizer and designer mulch.

The fertilizer is applied, grass starts to grow, and lawns are cut using mowers that bag clippings. Fresh grass clippings supply abundant nitrogen that can feed a lawn, but fortunately my neighbors are kind enough to put their clippings in plastic bags and throw them away with their trash. They do this because they've swallowed the story that grass clippings accumulate enough not only to choke their lawns, but to create enough thatch to build grass huts. I'm fortunate that they haven't swallowed the story that soil under an organically grown lawn has a profusion of organisms that rapidly break down clippings, which fertilizes grass naturally.

Fall, Winter, and Renewal

When the first tree leaves drop in the fall, my neighbors work very hard on my behalf, expunging every fallen leaf from their yards. This culminates in huge quantities of bagged leaves being left at the curb. Again, I'm quite fortunate that it escapes their notice that these bags of leaves resemble the bags of mulch that they bought in the spring. The difference, of course, is that the bags of leaves are free and are packed in rather unsightly trash bags.

Winter comes and goes, and the designer mulch my neighbors applied the previous spring finally breaks down. The timing is perfect for the cycle to begin again. So in April, they make their yearly pilgrimage to the garden center.

This cycle provides me with all the mulch and compost material I need. My yearly cycle coincides with theirs, with my hunting activity increasing as their waste volume increases. In the spring, their clippings mulch my flower and vegetable garden. In the fall, their tree leaves cover my garden beds for the winter. When they stop bagging their garden waste in the winter, the recycler in me goes into hibernation.

The only problem with my mulch gathering is that I have to drive around the neighborhood, weaving my way between trash and garbage cans to get to the golden gleanings left at the curb. I park next to bags of grass clippings or tree leaves and dash out to throw all the mulch I can into my station wagon before I'm noticed.

Sometimes I succeed; sometimes I fail.

When I fail, the following vignette usually takes place: The resident comes around from the back of the house and looks at me warily. To him, I have the lowliest profession in the world: not a trashman, but a trash-picker. He looks at me with complete disdain, while I sputter out, "Is it OK if I take your leaves? They make great mulch in my garden." After he gets over his surprise that I can speak an intelligible sentence, he smirks and says, "No, go ahead."

My neighbor returns to his backyard certain that he's just survived a close-up encounter with an escapee from an institution for the criminally insane.

If only my garden could understand the humiliation I go through to create the black, rich soil it contains. If only I could become invisible when I go out on my Sunday night raids. If only I didn't need the mulch at all.

But like vampires who abhor their deeds but cannot change, I go out week after week to prey upon my neighbors, and they can't help but feed my hunger.

Even now, as I commit these words to paper, the sun has set and I can hear the unmistakable sound of bags of leaves being placed at the curb. The old urge sweeps over me and I cannot restrain myself. You see, there are still a few square feet of my vegetable beds that contain no mulch.

Unlike Count Dracula, I can't disguise myself by changing into a bat. But last Halloween I bought a Bill Clinton mask; and, after the antics of Monicagate, I don't think he'll mind if he has to go through one more humiliation.

Plant Pirating 101

Tell the truth: If you're over the age of forty, shopping in general has become torture, and clothes shopping in particular is down there in Dante's ninth circle of hell. To my mind, bending over to plant twenty-five annuals is a lark, but bending over to try on twenty-five pairs of pants is agony.

I have such an abhorrence of shopping for garments that it's not surprising to see me walking around in old clothes that are held together by worn threads and fervent prayers.

When I was a kid, the gift I hated receiving the most was clothing. Footballs, golf balls, and board games sent me to heaven; clothes made me want to send the gift-giver in the other direction. However, after enduring almost fifty years of garment shopping, my most preferred gift is clothes. But since I have only a few gift-receiving occasions per year, I eventually have to expand my wardrobe using tremendous will power.

Although intellectually I know that I have to shop for clothes, the only way I can accomplish the task is by deceiving my nervous system.

Here's my methodology: I go to the local mall to have lunch at the food court. When I'm finished, I'm ready to hazard a walk past the clothing stores. Next comes the tough part: I have to walk through a department store to get to my car. As I near the men's clothing department, my stomach churns and my skin crawls. The door to the parking lot is just ahead. I make a furtive glance at the pants display, and, if I'm not overcome by hives or waves of nausea, I take a deep breath and force my legs to carry me into the world of cotton, wool, and polyester blends.

Only through a mix of self-hypnosis and sheer will do I manage to get through the ordeal of slipping on as many as six pairs of pants. And, as long as my new clothes neither fit like loose drapes nor tourniquets, they become my new wardrobe. My charge card is surrendered, I sign the appropriate receipts, and I escape for another two years.

Having explained my predicament, it won't surprise you that I've come up with another modus operandi for filling my closet. It's called "Shopping on the Run," and it works like this: You pick someone out of a crowd who closely matches your physique. If you admire items of clothing worn by the stranger, you stop, pay him or her a compliment, and make a monetary offer for the apparel you want. If the bid is accepted, you've added to your wardrobe without driving to a mall, parking, walking, trying on clothes, and paying top price.

What could be easier?

Some of you may think I'm not serious about this, so let me relate a personal experience. Recently, I admired a tie worn by a clerk at my local convenience store. It was adorned with cows in various colors and postures. The main color scheme was black and white, so I knew it would perfectly match my black pants and white shirts.

I complimented the clerk on his tie, made a $10 offer, it was accepted, and I expanded my wardrobe without a tortuous trip to a clothing store. "Shopping on the Run" worked like a dream.

The beautiful part of this strategy is that there's no embarrassment for you, since you stay fully clothed during the transaction; only the seller disrobes.

I wish I could take credit for this scheme, but for centuries, millions of gardeners have been acquiring their plants by "Shopping on the Run." I'm referring, of course, to how we procure the plants we admire in someone else's garden. During my lifetime, I don't think I've met a single avid gardener who hasn't asked a host or hostess for a cutting of a prized plant. But since gardeners have an even greater attachment to their plants than their clothes, they usually refuse to have their plants denuded by their avaricious visitors.

Accordingly, because they have no alternative to satisfy their horticultural yearnings, gardeners resort to the shady, botanical version of "Shopping on the Run," namely, "Plant Pirating." Although most of us have contemplated stealing cuttings from friends, neighbors, and public gardens, not everyone knows how to proceed. So, even though I promised not to make this book into a boring, gardening "how-to" diatribe, I feel it's only fair to give you the benefit of my experience.

Cutting kleptomania involves the following steps:

1. Cultivate one long, sharp thumbnail.
2. Be sure to stuff several small Baggies into the pockets of your pants before you visit a garden.
3. When the main contingent of visitors is occupying the attention of the homeowner, turn your back to the group, bend at the waist, and admire the prized specimen you fancy.
4. Use the age-old magician's method of diversion by staring at a bloom or branch you have in one hand, while you covertly snip a cutting from another branch using your sharpened thumbnail. This cutting should be no larger than the palm of your hand or it might be seen during the next step.
5. Hide the cutting by surrounding it with your fingers, and place it into a waiting Baggie in your pocket.
6. Fold over the Baggie to lock in humidity.
7. Gradually loosen your grip on the prized plant in the other hand and continue your "Plant Pirating" tour of the garden.

Admire, divert, snip, seal. What could be easier?

Now let's see, it's time to plan my next "Shopping on the Run" trip. For clothes, I've heard that employees at my nearby convenience store are wearing ties adorned with pictures of sandwich rolls. I think it would be the perfect accessory for my beige pants and white shirts.

And for plants, which one of you would like me to organize a tour of your garden next year?

A New Jersey Yankee
in Robert E. Lee's Court

It was neither the first orchid she had stolen, nor would it be the last.

She took the small *Dendrobium* out of her pocketbook and looked around her house for a place to set it down. This was never an easy task, because her orchids were everywhere: They hid windows, seized kitchen space, overran her coffee table, pushed toiletries aside, appropriated floor space, and hung from ceilings. Every bit of light — every photon — fell on her orchids. Aside from the natural light that came through windows, she had incandescent lights, fluorescent lights, and even sodium discharge lamps that made her home glow. In the evening, it looked like a new business using huge spotlights to attract customers.

Elaine Walters awoke at five o'clock every morning to water, fertilize, and groom a collection of over twelve hundred orchids. But even that amount didn't satisfy her. So, aside from her pirated plants, she imported them from around the world to take up residence in their new home; and it truly was *their* home, because she was their slave.

Her mania started when she was a teenager, shortly after her father died. She received a corsage from her senior prom date and was immediately smitten. Elaine couldn't take her eyes off the orchid, and by the end of the evening, her date was dancing with someone else, while she was flower fondling.

The next day, she bought her first potted orchids.

In college she had a new roommate every year, because no one could bear to stay in her dorm room jungle for more than two semesters. By the time she bought a house, she needed two moving vans: one for her orchids and one for everything else.

Every bit of extra income was used to buy orchids, lights for orchids, and books about orchids. In fact, any shelf that didn't hold plants was used for her sizeable library of orchid books.

One summer evening she was lying on her sofa, reading a newsletter from one of the thirty-seven orchid societies she had joined. Most of it contained information about growing techniques she already knew, so she skimmed quickly to the last page. And, just as she was about to put the newsletter down, she saw it: an account of how famed orchid expert Henry Graham had discovered a new species in a Georgia wildlife preserve. After verification, the plant was given the name *Galearis henriettae* in honor of Henry's wife, Henrietta.

Next to the column, there was a color photo of the plant. The new orchid had red flowers that were larger than its cousin, *Galearis spectabilis*, which had white and lavender flowers. Even its scent was reputed to be more powerful than any previously found *Galearis* species.

Elaine was transfixed by the picture for more than ten minutes.

The following day she started investigating, and learned that researchers were having trouble growing the new plant using tissue culture techniques; so no one knew when the new species would be available to orchid fanciers. And, although she knew that the plant had been discovered in Georgia, the exact location of the new orchid was kept secret.

She put the newsletter aside, disappointed that she'd never possess the new plant. Elaine closed her eyes and tried to relax, but couldn't erase the vision of the new, red-flowered orchid.

Then, something occurred to her and she sat up.

Elaine remembered attending a botanical symposium at Temple University where Graham was one of the speakers. He had used a map of Georgia to show where he was going to do field work in the coming year. Given Graham's limited area of exploration and the fact that the new orchid grew in the moss of limestone swamps, Elaine knew there was only one place where it could be located: The Laevigata Nature Preserve.

That's when she decided it was time for a vacation.

She got permission from her boss to take a week off, then started to make detailed plans for her expedition. Her packing list included hip waders, Wellie boots, large plastic bags, an extension ladder, buckets, anti-tick spray, a miner's helmet, Geological Survey Maps, a compass, and other items needed by a plant-napper.

Two weeks later, she was on the way from New Jersey to Alsophila, Georgia. After an overnight stop in Virginia, she drove due south toward the Laevigata Nature Preserve. Even if she had never heard of *Galearis henriettae*, this would have been a wonderful vacation, because Laevigata was known for its vast quantity and diversity of orchids.

Upon arrival in Alsophila, Elaine checked into a local motel, showered, then went to the entrance of the preserve to begin her search.

The first day, Elaine saw many orchids and mapped their locations, but didn't find the newly discovered plant. Day two was no better. And, after three days, she was exhausted from lack of sleep, tramping in swamps, and insect bites. She was starting to lose hope of ever finding *Galearis henriettae*.

On the morning of the fourth day, she awoke at dawn and reentered Laevigata. Elaine had divided her map into a grid to document where she had already searched. There was still one southern section Elaine hadn't explored, so she rode her van as close as she could, then took her gear and walked into the marshy forest. The sky was overcast, so she had to move slowly because of the dim light.

At mid-morning the clouds started to thin, making the floor of the forest brighter and allowing her to cover more ground.

Just before noon, she saw a small boggy area about two hundred yards ahead that was covered with moss. As Elaine got closer, the sun came out, and sent light streaming through the overhead canopy of leaves. The brightness blinded her for a moment, but her eyes adjusted and, up ahead, she saw red on the floor of the forest.

She began to run through the muck. Breathing hard, carrying her gear, she slipped and became muddied, then stood, walked quickly, coming closer, nearer. Finally she stopped, surrounded by a red carpet of flowers.

It was *Galearis henriettae*.

Elaine had never seen such beautiful orchids growing in the wild. The flowers were 1½"–2" across, and their scent was so powerful that the air smelled like a perfumery. She stared at the plants, not moving for several minutes. There were hundreds.

A fresh breeze blew against her face, awakening Elaine from a trance. She realized it was time to complete her work. So, with the care of a pediatric surgeon, she used her trowel to remove three plants from the marsh, then placed them in small plastic bags. She gathered her supplies and began the long walk back. After twenty steps, she turned around for one last look at the grouping of *Galearis henriettae*.

When Elaine reached her van, she placed the orchids in the safest places she could find and drove back to her motel room. She considered leaving for home, but couldn't forget the other orchids on the ground and in the trees of the nature preserve.

Thirty minutes later, she was back for more plants, promising herself that she'd stay for just a few more hours. Using the map that marked the locations of orchids she'd spotted the first three days, Elaine headed for her quarry. After making sure that no one could see her, she began placing orchids in dark plastic bags.

After three hours, she was filling her fifth bag when she heard a motor, then brakes. Through the dusk, Elaine saw an old man peering at her through a truck window.

She dropped her shovel and bag, waved at him, but he turned away and drove off.

It was time to go … fast.

She looked down and saw two bags, a shovel, a trowel, and more orchids.

Stuff the plants in the bag. Grab everything. Too much weight. Sling the bags over your shoulder. That's better.

Move. Left leg, then right leg, over again, over again. Look ahead. Ahead. It's slipping. It's slipping. Hold tighter. Tighter. Damn! The bag dropped. Don't leave it; pick it up. Pick it up. Back on your shoulder. That's it. That's it.

Breathing fast. Left, then right. Heavy legs, heavy bags.

Almost to van. Just ahead.

Everything down. Find the key, open the door. Now, everything inside. Shovel, trowel, two bags. Close the door.

Open the door. Open the door. Key in ignition. Turn it. Turn it. Turn over. Turn over. Turn over.

"Dammit. Flooded!"

Right foot off gas; wait a minute. A whole minute.

Sixty, fifty-nine, fifty-eight … twenty, nineteen … five, four, three, two …

Turn the key. Come on motor. Catch. Catch. Start. Start. Start.

That's it.

"Thank God!"

Forward, go forward. Getting dark. Good, good. One last curve, then out. Out of here and home. Get through the gate; just get there.

What's that? Lights ahead, turning lights. Lights on top, turning, spinning. A cop!

Stop. Stop. Turn around, around. Go slow, slow, like you forgot something.

Right. That's right. Got to be another way out. Maybe just wait or stay all night. Take the curve back. Head away from the cop. Good. Good.

Wait. More lights ahead, turning lights. Stop, stop, have to stop.

"Godammit! Godammit! You had to get more. So godamned greedy!"

Breathing hard, pulse fast, can't swallow. Here he comes. Act dumb, just act dumb.

The deputy reached her vehicle and looked through the window. She couldn't see him because of his blinding flashlight.

"Old Sam saw you digging up plants and called us," he said.

The deputy's light illuminated the plastic bags in the back of the van. He asked her to open the back door, then he removed the plants from each bag. There must have been two dozen orchids. Next, he asked her to open the well that held the spare tire. Once opened, he found two of the *Galearis henriettae* plants.

"You came from New Jersey, stole plants from our preserve, and thought you could get away with it, huh?" he asked.

She stuck to her plan and said, "You mean no one can take any plants from here?"

"R-i-g-h-t," he said, then laughed. "Well lady, you're under arrest, so here's your Miranda rights." He recited them, then said she could tell the sheriff how she wanted to plead. After taking her driver's license and registration card, he told her to drive slowly toward the exit and stop.

Elaine moved her van forward, with the deputy close behind. When they stopped next to the gate, the other deputy looked at her, then walked past and said, "Why can't these damned Yankees stay up North?"

Her mouth was as dry as sandpaper and her hands were sweaty. She looked out the windshield and noticed the old man who had seen her stealing orchids. He had a cell phone in his hand.

She was told to drive her van between the two police cars and follow them back to the sheriff's office.

That's where things got worse.

Elaine walked between the two deputies and stepped inside, where the air was a blue fog. It was Saturday night and the local jail was a hangout. There were ten men, and only the sheriff and two deputies wore uniforms. Most of them held lit cigarettes, despite the non-smoking sign on the door.

She laughed to herself. This was tobacco country, where tobacco not only thickened the air, but also wallets.

Elaine gazed around the room. The walls were an ugly yellow, and in one corner there was a wall calendar of a nude woman on a motorcycle.

When she looked at the men, she realized that every pair of eyes was studying her. Some of them had three days of stubble and looked grisly. One man smiled at her, but had eyes as cold as steel. His teeth were yellow, and a few were missing.

The same revolting man stopped smiling, then said, "What you got here, Sheriff? This here the Yankee from New Jersey?"

"Yeah, that's her," Sheriff May replied.

Another man who was holding a bottle of beer said, "What's the matter lady, ain't you got enough plants to steal up North? You have to come down here and steal ours, too?"

The men continued to smoke and stare. She stood next to the sheriff's desk and felt about as safe as a lamb in a slaughterhouse.

One man with greasy hair and a stained T-shirt said, "Hey Sheriff, I ever tell you about my great, great grandfather Matthew?"

"No, Nathan, what about him?"

"He was at Second Manassas, during the War of Northern Aggression."

Oh God, Elaine thought, *I've walked straight into the movie "Deliverance."*

"It's a fact; he fought in a Georgia regiment that butchered some boys from New Jersey. He killed a colonel and got his sword. It's over our mantelpiece at home.

"We sure are proud of it, although it hasn't gotten much use lately."

Everyone burst into laughter.

"Yeah, we can laugh now, but Matthew had it pretty bad. He came back from the war and found his house burned out of existence by that bastard Sherman.

"Before his boys set it afire, they stole everything worth anything."

Nathan stopped talking and looked at Elaine. He raised an arm and pointed at her, saying, "And now we got another Yankee down here doing more thieving."

Elaine felt everyone's penetrating glare, and began to fear that she wouldn't survive the night. Feeling lightheaded, she put one hand on the sheriff's desk, then realized that the other hand was shaking.

She peered at the sheriff and their eyes met. He looked down at her trembling hand, then said, "OK boys, time to let me do my job. Y'all go home now."

A few of them protested, but they all stood and took one more look at her on the way out.

"Guess you won't be paying us another visit any time soon!" Nathan said, making his friends laugh again.

Once they were gone, the sheriff had her sit down, then said, "You'll have to excuse my friends. There are still people down here a little crazy when it comes to the Civil War.

"Well, let's get this over with. Did the deputies tell you your rights?"

She nodded without looking up.

"Well," he said, "let me tell you like it is. It's fine if you want to wait until tomorrow or the next day for us to find you a lawyer, but I think this can all be settled in the morning. You and I both know what you did. Sam saw you in the act, and his cousin's the judge around here. I think I can smooth this over with the head of Laevigata, so you'll probably get off with just a fine.

"Y'know, you're lucky you ended up in my jail, and not in the one on the other side of Laevigata. That sheriff's plain mean, and he's not a family man like me. I got two daughters about your age.

"So, it's up to you. You can answer a few questions tonight or wait around until we unearth a lawyer."

"No, Sheriff," she replied, "it's OK; I'll answer your questions."

After ten minutes the sheriff had finished, then asked, "You want to call anybody?"

In a barely audible voice, Elaine said "No, thank you, sir."

He escorted her to a jail cell and clanged the door shut. Once Elaine was behind bars and left alone, she began to relax. She hadn't murdered anyone or robbed a bank, so she wasn't going to spend the rest of her life in jail. On the other hand, if she weren't let off with just a fine, it would be difficult to explain her absence to her friends, family, and boss.

After she sat on the bed, something occurred to her: She had put the third *Galearis henriettae* in her glove compartment. And, since she had already surrendered her insurance and registration cards, they probably wouldn't search there for plants.

Focusing on the orchid calmed her. So, seven hundred miles from home, in a Southern jail cell, Elaine actually fell asleep.

The next morning, Sheriff May and Mr. Newman, the head of the preserve, spoke with her and reviewed the information on the police report. Although Newman was incensed by what she had done, he agreed with the sheriff's suggestion to let her go home after paying a $600 fine and replanting the orchids. She quickly agreed to do both, and, by the end of the day, was released from custody.

Elaine left the sheriff's office, threw her belongings into the van, and left town. She drove north, widening the distance between her and the town that had been, perhaps still was, part of the Confederacy.

After fifteen minutes, she steered to the side of the road and stopped. Elaine made sure there were no police cars nearby, then turned off the motor and slipped a key into the locked glove compartment. The small door swung open and the third *Galearis henriettae* spilled out.

Elaine gasped and reached for the plant, cradling it in her hands. She stared at the new orchid and felt sheer ecstasy. After checking that the plant was unharmed, she returned it to the glove compartment, then started her van and slowly drove away.

Elaine turned on the radio, but couldn't concentrate on anything except her new orchid. After staring at the glove compartment, she thought about the last five days. In her mind, the arrest, the dangerous men at the sheriff's office, the night in jail, and the fine were more than outweighed by the new orchid. She felt neither shame, nor regret, nor penitence. What she felt was inner peace.

The Holy Grail was in her glove compartment, bound for New Jersey and a new home.*

---

*This story is a work of fiction, but it was inspired by actual events. All plots, themes, dates, events, locations, organizations, persons, and characters contained in this material are completely fictional. Any resemblance to any locations, organizations, persons, or characters, real or fictional, living or deceased, is entirely coincidental and unintentional.

"Anybody have any tranquilizers for Wolk?"

8

FLOWER SHOWS
PART TWO

A Grand Experience

I HAD NEVER COMMITTED A CRIME before, but winning the Philadelphia Flower Show Grand Sweepstakes Trophy was pushing me in that direction.

One of my three essential artistic entries was locked in a flower shop, and I didn't have the key. My choices were to break and enter or end my quest. I made my decision: Winning the silver trophy was worth the risk of being caught and thrown in jail. As I pushed against the door, I looked up and noticed that my dark cloud from two years before was directly overhead.

After my flower show adventures — and misadventures — from 1993, I continued exhibiting. In 1994, I doubled my point total, winning fifteen blue ribbons and another daffodil rosette. I had enough points to reach fifth place in the horticultural standings, but the process was exhausting. After entering seventy-five pots over three different judging days, I didn't even want to think about 1995.

But that feeling didn't last.

By midsummer I decided to compete for the Grand Sweepstakes Trophy — an award given to the exhibitor who accumulates the most points in the artistic and horticultural classes combined (see sidebar, page 56).* To win it, an exhibitor has to enter at least three entries in both areas. Of course, I wouldn't have a problem providing the required

---

*The point total for each exhibitor depends on the number and type of ribbons they win, with blue ribbons having the highest value. All the points that an exhibitor earns are added together to determine who wins the Grand Sweepstakes Award.

number of horticultural entries, but artistic entries were another matter. I had never produced a single display.

After a bit of research, I learned that artistic entries varied tremendously: from flower arrangements; to pressed flowers; to the niche classes, which were interpretations of a theme in a limited space. (For example, in one class exhibitors had to depict the theme "Paper Dolls" in a space of approximately one cubic foot.)

Winning the Horticultural Sweepstakes was out of the question for someone with my limited resources. In 1993 and 1994, Ray Rogers and Ken Selody, respectively, had each won the award, and they had at least ten times more greenhouse space than I. In 1995, it was rumored that Mr. and Mrs. Hamilton, with even more resources, were trying to win it.

So, winning the Grand Sweepstakes trophy was my mission, and my competition would be formidable: Rosemarie Vassalluzzo, a champion who had won the award for twelve straight years.

From the beginning, I knew I'd have to win a lot more points than Rosemarie in the horticultural classes to make up for her absolute superiority in the artistic categories. An accurate comparison would be that I had the artistic expertise of a three-year-old finger painter, while she could have used dried flowers to recreate Leonardo Da Vinci's *Last Supper*.

Realizing this, I decided to take a flower-arranging course simply to avoid humiliation.

In the late summer of 1994, I obtained bulbs, seeds, and rooted cuttings that would produce most of my entries. Approximately twenty-five older plants would be used as well. Since many of my entries would be potted bulbs, I'd need perfect weather conditions to maximize output. If everything peaked at the right time, I'd have 130–150 horticultural entries.

Every year has its own meteorological personality that stays in a gardener's memory. The winter of 1993-94 had been so cold, that the following year I decided to use foam board to insulate my cold frames that contained potted bulbs. As it turned out, my precautions were unwarranted because the winter of 1994-95 was one of the mildest in history.

After one warm spell in January, I opened a cold frame and found several pots of *Crocus* starting to show yellow buds. Since the show was two months away, I suspended their growth by covering them with chopped ice that I made each morning. I also had to keep track of another eighty pots of bulbs and make sure they stayed at the proper stages of growth. Each had to be brought into the greenhouse on the appropriate day to ensure peak bloom for the show.

By February, my greenhouse had plants on the floor, on growing benches, on shelves, and in hanging baskets. In addition, I had indoor plants under fluorescent light units in our den. As the flower show approached, my home and greenhouse began to look like a retail plant shop. Each day, I got up ninety minutes early to care for 125 potted plants.

With fifteen days to go, I had forty pots that were coming along too fast, so I slowed their growth by putting them outdoors or in my unheated garage.

My artistic entries included two miniature dried flower arrangements that were no more than five inches in any direction. The third was a medium niche entry in a three-dimensional space that was approximately twenty-four inches on each side. Since the theme for this largest entry was "Color Magic," I decided to make a fresh flower arrangement in a magic hat with a synthetic magician's hand and wand suspended above the hat.

Friday, March 3rd: It usually takes thirty minutes to groom each plant for exhibit, but since flowering bulbs are at their peak for such a short time, they can't be groomed until the night before entry. An extreme example is *Iris reticulata*, which is at its peak for about four hours indoors. So exhibitors do their best to make sure those four hours occur when the judges walk by.

The night before the first judging day I had only groomed seven pots by 7:30PM, when I got a call from a *Washington Post* reporter. He said that I had pre-registered more plants than anyone else and that a lot was expected of me.* I talked with him for thirty minutes, then panicked because I had another thirty-three pots to prepare. After pleading for assistance, my wife and daughter agreed to help groom

---

*Exhibitors pre-register entries in mid-January by sending the Pennsylvania Horticultural Society a list of the plants they intend to enter in the show.

pots until midnight. I stayed up all night and by the next morning had forty pots ready for entry.

Saturday, March 4th: Four assistants arrived at five o'clock. After helping me load my plants into a rented truck, they followed me to the show. At the unloading dock each pot was carefully removed, but when I backed up my rented truck, I heard the terrible sound of metal against metal. Jumping out, I discovered that I had scraped the station wagon next to me.

So there I was at the dock, it was 7:30AM, I hadn't entered a single plant, and I had gotten into an accident. The owner of the car was missing, but since it was unlocked, we were able to release the emergency brake and push it out of the way. Some ridiculous bystanders actually suggested that I summon the police and file a report before entering my plants in the show.

Once inside, my luck improved. There were two grooming tables reserved for me, and I had my own passer, Ellie Lloyd, for the bulb classes. The only distraction was a *Washington Post* photographer who repeatedly took flash photos while I completed last minute grooming. I got my miniature dried flower arrangement passed and was able to enter thirty-nine pots before the nine thirty deadline.

During judging, the *Washington-Post* reporter talked with me for an hour. After my interview, I found the woman whose car I had hit. Like most exhibitors, she was too excited about her flower show entries to care about something as trivial as a dented car.

When the judges finished, I scurried around and found that I had won numerous ribbons, including six blues. Even my first artistic entry won an honorable mention ribbon. So far, I had a 150-point lead on Rosemarie.

Monday, March 6th: During the afternoon, I bought fresh flowers and went to my flower-arranging teacher's shop. Although it wasn't open for business, she left the back door unlocked so I could use her equipment to create my "Color Magic" entry for Tuesday. I entered at half past three and finished by five o'clock. Then I loaded my car and started to leave the parking lot, but a feeling of dread came over me. I frantically looked for all my materials and realized that I had left the magician's hat and other props in the flower shop. I went to the back door, only to find that I had locked it.

I had a big lead over Rosemarie, but if I didn't get all three artistic entries into the show, I wouldn't qualify for the Grand Sweepstakes Award.

For a minute, I was too unnerved to figure a way out my dilemma. But gradually, I calmed down and considered my options. If I did nothing, my quest was over. I could have a million point lead, but it wouldn't matter if I didn't get this artistic entry into the show. My other choice was to figure out a way to break into the flower shop. In a moment, I made up my mind: I was going to break and enter.

I examined the locked door and noticed that it had six window-panes, three of which were covered with plywood that was nailed in place from the inside. If I could find something heavy enough, I'd be able to force the plywood away from the door. Scouring the area, I found a log of firewood on the side of the flower shop. Before I used it, my eyes darted everywhere to be certain no one was watching. I didn't see anyone but was filled with apprehension that an unseen police officer was watching me. Before my fear overcame my resolve, I started to push against the plywood. Within thirty seconds, I had made enough space to fit my arm through the window and unlock the door. Back in the shop, I found my paraphernalia and quickly placed them into my car. After repairing the door the best I could, I bolted from the lot.

That evening, with the help of family and friends, I prepared fifty pots. The weather report predicted that temperatures would stay above freezing that night, so I packed most of the entries in my rented truck.

I even got two heavenly hours of sleep.

Tuesday March 7th: Up at 4:30AM, I checked that I had every item I'd need, including entry cards. When an exhibitor enters a plant in a horticultural category, two 4" X 6" cards are needed. They must contain the exhibitor's name, address, phone number, and horticultural organization on one side, and the class number and the plant's Latin name on the other. When I checked my cards, I thought the pile looked thin for fifty entries. Sure enough, there was only one card for each entry. My wife had prepared the cards the night before, but I had neglected to tell her that I needed two cards for each plant. Fortunately, one of my friends agreed to print a second set.

By 6:25AM we were on the road, but after five minutes I had a terrible feeling that I had forgotten something. I couldn't think of what it might be, so I didn't stop the caravan of cars that was following me.

We got to the flower show without incident, but at the unloading dock a guard stared at me with a dead serious expression. He looked down at his feet and walked in my direction.

"Are you Art Wolk?" he asked.

"Yeah, why?"

"I'm sorry to tell you this, but your wife called and told us that you left all your entry cards at home."

I stared at him in disbelief and shook my head.

The guard saw my reaction and tried to calm my nerves, saying, "Your wife left the cards next to the front door so someone could go back to get them."

"Thanks," I said, and he slunk away.

I felt like I'd just been punched in the abdomen, but I had to make a snap decision. If I sent one of my four helpers back home for the cards, she might not return in time. That being the case, I decided to have one of my perennial assistants, Joan Hemphill, prepare cards for the next two-and-a-half hours.

When we got indoors, there were more problems: Neither a passer nor grooming tables were available, so I had to expend vital minutes to obtain both. I also sent someone to get a pack of blank entry cards. When they arrived, Joan started to fill them out.

The person who was especially invaluable was my passer, Ellie Lloyd. She not only helped make out cards and get bulb entries passed, but she had a tranquilizing influence on me. Ellie saw how nervous I was, so she told me to get my artistic entry passed while they worked on the cards.

At the artistic staging area, I found that I had been given the last stall. Since the only entrance to the back of the medium niches was at the opposite end, I had to make repeated long-distance runs, back and forth, to check each adjustment.* Luckily, the mat boards I had prepared for the background fit perfectly. I placed the magic hat and flower arrangement in their proper locations, then started to hang the

---

*Medium niche exhibitors construct their entries from the back and check them from the front.

magician's hand. I finished within ten minutes, had my entry passed, and ran back to the horticultural area. It was now 7:50AM, meaning I had just one hundred minutes left.

I decided to enter my best plants first. But when I began, someone from the artistic categories tapped me on the shoulder. She said that there was a problem with some sickly looking flowers in my artistic entry. I moaned and ran back to my "Color Magic" entry, where a passer told me that two of my roses had blackened petals. I had extra cut flowers, so I simply replaced the bad flowers. The entry was passed for the second time; then I dashed back to my plants

It was eight o'clock, and not one single horticultural entry had been passed. I had ninety minutes to enter fifty pots. I started grooming plants, Ellie passed the bulb entries, and my friends rushed around the exhibit floor to get my "non-bulb" entries passed. At nine-thirty we were all exhausted, but had managed to get forty-nine of the fifty pots into the show.

Although my artistic entry didn't win a ribbon, I won six more blue ribbons in the horticultural classes as well as a rosette for the best entry in the daffodil classes.* By the end of the day, I had over a 300-point lead on Rosemarie.

My last artistic entry, to be entered on Thursday, was a miniature dried flower arrangement destined for a class named "In Vogue." In spite of all my preparation, I felt anxious when I read the exhibitor's booklet. It stated that my entry was supposed to be a "design." After seeing the artistic creations that had won awards that week, I was convinced that what judges wanted and what I produced were in different realms. So I imagined the worst possibility: that my entry wasn't appropriate for the category and wouldn't be passed.

I decided to call Lucie Steele, the chairperson of the class. After hearing my concern, she suggested that I show her my entry on Wednesday morning.

---

*To win the Grand Sweepstakes Award, the three required artistic entries don't have to win a ribbon; they just have to be passed (entered) into the competition. Even so, they must follow the rules for each competitive class or passers won't allow them into the show.

Wednesday, March 8th: At eight o'clock, I drove into Philadelphia to let Steele evaluate my entry. It was a miniature dried flower arrangement shaped like a standard, meaning it looked like a small tree with a straight trunk and a sphere at the top. Within five seconds, Steele said it was fine.

I was relieved; but knowing everything that could go wrong, I wished I could enter my arrangement immediately, instead of taking it home and coming back the next morning. I had such a big lead that the only thing that could stop me from winning the trophy would be my failure to get this essential third artistic entry into the show.

On Wednesday night, I called Joan (my "entry card savior") and asked her to follow me to the show in her car. She would be my "insurance" in case my car had problems. Joan agreed to meet me at six o'clock at my house. I went to sleep that night not knowing what could go wrong, but certain that something would.

Thursday, March 9th: During the evening, my dark cloud returned: freezing rain came down all night and coated everything in ice. I awoke at five o'clock and leisurely showered, dressed, and ate breakfast. At 5:55 AM I went to my car, only to find it completely encased in ice. To make matters worse, both door locks were frozen shut and my key wouldn't go into either lock.

I banged on the door to loosen the ice, but it didn't budge. Next, I went inside to heat the key, but that didn't work either.

It was quarter past six, I couldn't get into my car, and Joan was late. I assumed that she was also stymied by the ice. Again, I tried heating my key at our stove. This time the key went into the door on the driver's side, but wouldn't turn. On the passenger side, the key went in, turned, and at long last I unlocked the door. I sighed with relief and began loading my car. By the time I finished, Joan arrived.

We drove to the show without incident, then parked and took everything inside. Within thirty minutes, I set up my artistic entry and it was passed.

Although I had fifty horticultural entries to prepare for Friday, I stayed at the show to see if I'd win a ribbon. What I hadn't realized previously was how long it took artistic judges to complete their work. In the horticultural classes, judges move quickly, spending no more than ten minutes to review a class with as many as twenty-five entries;

but the artistic judges moved about as fast as oozing mud, taking approximately ninety minutes to judge six entries. I came back every twenty minutes to see if they had finished, but it seemed as if their shoes were glued to the floor.

Finally, they moved on, but it took another twenty minutes before the ribbons were awarded and the judges' comments were posted.

I had received another honorable mention.

The judges thought my arrangement was somewhat traditional for the "In Vogue" theme. I was so new to artistic competition that I didn't know what was traditional or avant-garde. It was only after years of studying artistic composition as a photographer that I began to understand why certain entries were better than mine. But back in 1995, I didn't have the least idea why one of my competitors won the blue ribbon. For a few minutes I was miffed, but then I mentally stepped back and felt pure relief when I realized that I had completed all prerequisites for the Grand Sweepstakes Award.

That day, Rosemarie showed real class when she congratulated me. I felt bad that I was ending her run, but she thanked me for releasing her "from the insanity. Twelve years is enough!" Rosemarie also said she was "glad that a real gardener beat [her]." We looked each other in the eye and knew we didn't have to say the next sentence — that she was glad a non-gardening "gardener" didn't win.

Later that night, I toyed with the idea of not pushing myself to groom the entries I had aimed for Friday's judging, but then I thought I might have a chance of winning another trophy for placing second in the Horticultural Sweepstakes. So, I prepared all fifty entries and only got 1½ hours of sleep.

Friday, March 10th: On this final day of judging, everything went as planned. My entries garnered nine blues and another rosette in the *Narcissus* classes. For the week, I had received ninety-two ribbons, twenty-one of which were blues or rosettes. My final point total was 838 to Rosemarie's 338.

Saturday, March 11th: The best part of flower show week was having my wife and daughter with me during the awards banquet. I had to admit that they each deserved a Super Grand Sweepstakes Award for enduring all the turmoil.

It turned out that I missed winning the runner-up Horticultural

Sweepstakes Award by a mere fifteen points, but that didn't upset me because it wasn't my original goal. The Grand Sweepstakes Trophy was the last to be awarded, so even though I was 99% certain I had won, there was still room for doubt — perhaps an unknown exhibitor had slipped past me without my knowledge.

First they announced the runner-up, and when everyone heard "Rosemarie Vassalluzzo," there were gasps; then they called me to the podium to receive the silver trophy.

When the ceremonies were over, many people congratulated me and asked what I'd do for an encore in 1996. Given my state of exhaustion after all the work and near-catastrophes, I didn't even want to think about the following year.

In the end, I told them I'd let them know ... after four weeks of sleep.

The Colder the Better

Although I won the Grand Sweepstakes Award again in 1996, my three artistic entries were so bad that I was single-handedly responsible for a change in the rules. That year, two of my three entries were dioramas, or miniature scenes. I thought they looked dandy; the judges and Flower Show Committee thought otherwise. So, after my ill-fated attempt at floral artistry, they forbid dioramas forevermore in the classes I had entered. The most accurate statement of my artistic ability back then was that as an artistic exhibitor, I was a wonderful horticulturist. In other words, I had no understanding of the artistic side of flower shows.

Having said that, I should also mention that for certain artistic judges, the reverse seemed to be true: One panel of judges in 1996 wasn't familiar with the gardening side of horticulture as I knew it. That year, one of my three artistic entries was a miniature compost pile entered in a class named "Recycling." While it was being judged, a clerk approached me because the judges had a question: they didn't understand how a compost pile had anything to do with recycling!

I was shocked, but explained the composting process. The clerk showed no sign of comprehension, but relayed my words to the judges. To this day, I don't know if they understood the traditional gardening practice of recycling leaves, soil, and manure to produce a natural garden fertilizer.

As I learned in 1996, flower show exhibiting had an artistic yin and a horticultural yang that rarely intersected. I decided that my contentment lay on the yang side. So, although my itch for Grand Sweepstakes trophies had been scratched, horticultural blue ribbons still enthralled me.

To win as many as possible, I invented a way to provide the perfect growing conditions for potted bulbs.

Many gardeners know that heating cables can be used to raise soil temperature. They're pre-set to 70°F, which is too warm for root formation and flower stem extension of most spring-blooming bulbs; 48°F is ideal. I knew that if I could provide the right temperatures under the potted bulbs in my cold frames, I had a good chance of producing gorgeous entries. After a bit of creative planning, I bought refrigeration thermostats and had an electrician provide power to the thermostats that, in turn, controlled when the heating cables clicked on inside my cold frames.

My idea worked better than I had imagined. Many of the potted bulbs began to send up foliage and shoots while still inside the cold frames. By maintaining ideal soil temperatures, both foliage and flowers were at the perfect height. In effect, I was forcing the bulbs in my cold frames with minimal effort.

But unfortunately, there was a problem: In February it became too warm. In fact, before the month was over I saw cabbage white butterflies in my backyard. Somehow, I had to slow down my bulbs or I would have a superb flower show at home, weeks before the one in Philadelphia.

While searching for a solution, it occurred to me that a pattern had emerged: If it were an odd-numbered year, I would have calamities before and during the Philadelphia Flower Show. In 1993, there was a falling clerk, a dying car, and a blizzard. In 1995, there was an ice storm, forgotten entry cards, and breaking into a flower shop. In 1997, there was summer in February.

At first, I placed the pots outside the frames, hoping that would help, but outdoor temperatures continued to climb.

Not surprisingly, two days before the show I had sixteen pots that were perfect, meaning they had peaked too soon. To make matters worse, the high temperature that day was projected to hit 74°F. I needed to think fast or all sixteen pots would miss the show entirely.

I had the day off from work, so as soon as my wife drove to work, I removed half the food from our refrigerator and replaced it with the smallest potted bulbs.

Next, I gathered ice chests, put potted bulbs inside, and surrounded them with crushed ice. This worked fine for the medium-sized entries, but I was still left with large pots of tulips and daffodils.

After a few minutes, I hatched another plan: I packed my station wagon with the rest of the potted bulbs and went to my local convenience store. Before then, I had never said one word to the manager, but this was no time to be shy. I walked up to her and explained my predicament. She guessed where the conversation was headed and said, "So what do you want to do, put your pots in my refrigeration room?" Without hesitating I said she was right, and mentioned that I'd give her a ticket to the flower show in return for her assistance.

Luckily, she assented. So before she had a chance to change her mind, I started hauling in my large pots of tulips, daffodil, and whatever other potted bulbs had to be cooled. The conditions in her refrigeration room were a perfect 38°F. I'd heard of other exhibitors using refrigeration to suspend plant growth, but was always warned that foliage would start to fade in the dark conditions of a refrigerator. Fortunately, I didn't have that problem, because the lights in the convenience store's walk-in refrigerator were on twenty-four hours a day.

Now, finally, I didn't care about the high outdoor temperatures. All the pots aimed for the first Saturday of the show were in suspended animation.

I knew I was going to do well before I entered a single pot. As I brought my entries into the flower show, another excellent bulb forcer looked at my pots and waved me away, as if to say, "I can't win blue ribbons against those entries, so take them back home."

She was right; I succeeded as never before.

I entered forty-eight pots of bulbs and twenty-three received blue ribbons as well as two rosettes. Of the remaining pots, many received red (second-place) ribbons. Only one other exhibitor received more blue ribbons that year, but she had about thirty-times more greenhouse space than I.

After the show was over, I began to take a broader view of the competition. I had won many awards that gave me feelings of accomplishment, but I also realized that there was something even more important taking place. While everyone else endures winter's wrath, exhibitors grow dazzling springtime flowers. The beauty and aroma, surrounding us in an ever-increasing sensory display, is too much for us to hoard. So we take our flowers to the show in Philadelphia to share our stolen spring with you.

Just a few words of warning, though: When you visit competitive flower shows like the one in Philadelphia, be sure to stay clear of certain exhibitors moving around like roadrunners with potted bulbs under their wings. And, don't bother to ask any of them how one goes about exhibiting in flower shows, because most of us are too frantic to be intelligible.

Besides, would you really want to start an addiction that couldn't be cured even by a lengthy stay at the Betty Ford Center?

"This is Miss America...you'll be teaching her how to plant bulbs."

9

GARDEN TELEVISION
AND MAGAZINES

A Really Odd Couple:
Teaching Miss America
to Plant Bulbs on TV

WOMEN IN BATHING SUITS — glamorous women — with long legs, long hair, and long strides. Right above me. Smiling, stunning, goddesses. I was fifteen-years-old, sitting next to the runway at a Miss America pageant, full of hormones and full of insecurity.

Fantasies consumed me. The idea of touching a single contestant, even holding her hand, seemed impossible. But I dreamt that perhaps someday I'd meet a Miss America, hold her hand, and, and, ...

"Your Miss America for 1965 is Vonda Van Dyke!" Burt Parks yelled.

My head cleared and my fantasies drifted away.

Forget it Wolk, I thought to myself, *this is as close as you'll ever get to a Miss America. And touching her? You'll have a better chance of touching Venus.*

Or so I thought.

****

Three decades pass. I marry, become a father, and a garden lecturer.

When the Miss America pageant airs every September, I never watch. Sure, the women are beautiful and talented, but I can't stand the interviews. Some of the judges, and perhaps most of America, want each contestant to describe how she'll stop world hunger, the spread of disease, and put an end to war. Some women play the game. Some keep their dignity.

So I forget my teenage fantasy.

Or so I thought.

****

"Hello, is this Art Wolk?" a television producer asked in 1994.

"Yeah, I'm Art Wolk, who's this?"

"My name is Lee Heh Margolies and I'm a Discovery Channel producer. I see that you're a bulb specialist and that you'll be teaching a class nearby."

"That's right."

"Well, the TV show I produce, *Home Matters*, teaches women how to do projects in and around the home. I think you could help us do a segment about bulb planting."

My mind raced. This wasn't really happening, was it?

Quickly, I said, "Actually, we could probably do a segment about bulb forcing in pots and another on planting bulbs in the ground."

"That sound like a good idea," Margolies said.

"So I'll be teaching a TV audience how to plant bulbs?"

"Well yes, indirectly. But actually you'll be teaching Susan Powell, the 1981 Miss America, to plant bulbs."

Brain-lock set in. I didn't hear anything after the words, "Miss America."

"Hello, Art? Are you still there?"

"Uh, yeah, who did you say?"

"Susan Powell."

"And she was what?"

"Miss America in 1981."

This was becoming surreal. I remembered the Miss America pageant, the runway, the smiles, the legs, the fantasy ...

"Art ... Art ..."

"Huh? Oh, yeah, I'm here."

"Let's talk about location. Is there a beautiful garden nearby where we could do the taping next week?"

"Well, Longwood Gardens would be ideal, but since it's one of the world's premier public gardens, I don't think we'd be able to ..."

"Leave that to me," she interrupted.

Ten minutes later she called me back and said that everything was arranged. In six days I was going to Longwood Gardens to teach a Miss America about bulb gardening. I marveled that Lee Heh had obtained permission so easily.

After our phone conversation, her name stuck in mind: I knew I had heard it before. I decided to do some research and eventually discovered, and remembered, that she was the daughter of then Congresswoman Marjorie Margolies-Mezvinsky. Back in 1970, Lee Heh had been the first foreign-born child adopted by a single parent in the United States.

And there was more: In 1976 Lee Heh had accompanied her mother to the Democratic National Convention in New York City. One of the most intimidating men at the convention was Mayor Richard Daley from Chicago. In 1968, when the convention took place in his hometown, the police forcibly cleared anti-Vietnam War protestors from the streets, injuring many. Most people wouldn't have dared to mention the unrest to Daley. But as a twelve-year-old, Lee Heh had no difficulty confronting him about the 1968 convention. He told her that the problems were all an invention of the press. Soon thereafter, word spread about Lee Heh's conversation with Daley, and it became the laugh of the convention among both delegates and the media.

The story made me understand why she had been able to arrange our videotaping at Longwood Gardens so quickly. Obviously, Lee Heh wasn't the type of person who was easily intimidated.

On the other hand, the prospect of appearing on TV with a Miss America certainly intimidated me. To calm my nerves, I decided to hunt for information about Susan, and was happy to learn that she had sung an opera aria during the talent competition of the Miss America contest. That reduced my anxiety, because I'd been an opera-lover since the age of thirteen.

On the appointed morning, I loaded my car with bulbs, pots, soil mix, and shovels, then drove to Longwood Gardens. After unloading everything, I met the cameraman, soundman, and Margolies. I had made the mistake of assuming that someone with Margolies commanding phone presence would be physically intimidating as well, but she was barely five feet tall.

I looked around for Susan and finally spotted her near a flowerbed. She looked up, smiled, and walked toward me. Powell introduced herself and we shook hands.

In one sense, I realized a fantasy by actually holding a Miss America's hand. But in another sense, I realized how ridiculous my teenage fantasy had been. Susan may have been very attractive, but she was also an unassuming, easygoing person, not a Greek goddess.

A Longwood Gardens employee led us to the "Idea Garden," which looked exactly like a suburban backyard. After she left, I noticed that the camera was being set up to record us planting bulbs in a pristine lawn. With great effort, I managed to convince the crew that digging up a lawn wouldn't exactly endear us to Longwood's staff, so they reluctantly moved to an empty flowerbed.

While the production team prepared for taping, I asked Susan if she had continued her opera career. She was surprised that I knew about her background, but I mentioned that I was an opera fan as well as a librarian and that the information was easy to find. Before long, we were singing together and all my nervousness disappeared.

When the team was ready to begin taping, a small microphone was clipped to the shirt inside my sweater, and the producer discussed the scene with us. There was no script, so we simply reviewed the content of each take.

I began by explaining what bulbs are and how they're planted. Susan asked the proper questions, and we finished the take without any mistakes. I thought, *Great, this is going to be fast and easy.*

"*NO*," the soundman said emphatically, "the microphone was rubbing against Art's sweater and distorting the sound."

After adjusting my microphone, we started again and produced another excellent take. "*NO*," the soundman said again, "the birds were too noisy." The third take bothered the cameraman. I was casting too much of a shadow on Susan. On the fourth take, the producer didn't like that I was smiling at the camera; only Susan was supposed to do that. By then, the crouch I was in was taking its toll. My knees were beginning to ache, so if we didn't get the next take right, my career in television was going to be awfully short-lived.

Luckily, the fifth take made the film crew happy.

This part of the segment would be less than one minute long on TV, but had taken forty-five minutes to setup and shoot. I soon learned that for every *minute* you see of a "how-to" program on TV, there's usually an *hour* of preparation and taping.

Next, we set up for the bulb-forcing segment. But if the birds and sweater were a problem in the first segment, they were nothing compared to the power saws and lawn mowers that started during the second. Lee Heh dispatched us to ask the Longwood workmen to stop what they were doing since the Discovery Channel was taping.

Incredibly, they complied.

After another thirty minutes, a somber looking, tall, muscular supervisor appeared and complained that his workers had jobs to complete and that we were stopping them from getting their work done.

"When will you be finished?" he demanded.

"In forty-five minutes," Lee Heh replied.

"But we have work to get done!"

"We'll just be forty-five minutes," Lee Heh repeated.

This went on and on, with Lee Heh doing the broken record routine. Finally the supervisor said, "I'll just have to see my superiors about this!" and off he stomped.

Lee Heh didn't seem to break a sweat over this encounter. After all, who was this guy compared to Mayor Daley?

My reaction was quite different: I was certain that we'd be thrown out of Longwood Gardens at any moment. So naturally, I made my first mistake on the next take.

I hadn't made the yearly timetable of bulb forcing clear to Susan; so she ended one segment by saying, "We can have these wonderful fresh flowers in our house year-round."

I said, "That's right," but then realized the mistake we'd made.

When the cameraman stopped filming, I explained to Susan and Lee Heh that spring-blooming bulbs are available only in the fall, that they need autumn's cool soil conditions to start rooting, and that they're only forced into bloom in the winter and early spring. They understood my explanation; then we did one more take — without the error — and were finished for the day.

We had taped for seven hours to produce what would ultimately be about eight minutes on TV. I was exhausted, but relieved that we had concluded our work without being ejected.

On my way home from Longwood Gardens, I had difficulty believing that all of that day's events had really taken place. I remembered the Miss America pageant, and the fifteen-year-old boy who had contemplated the impossibility of meeting a Miss America.

Or so I had thought.

****

After the taping at Longwood, the spring and summer seemed to drag on endlessly.

Finally, the bulb-forcing segment aired in early October. My family and I sat expectantly in front of the TV to see my nationwide debut. I thought it went very well, but when we watched it again on videotape, I realized that they had left in the "year-round" statement. There was Susan, saying that you could force bulbs anytime of the year, and there I was, agreeing!

Of course, there was nothing that could be done at that point. At first I was upset, but in the end I only saw the positives. After all, how many gardeners get on television to show a Miss America — and America — how to plant bulbs?

I also realized something else: I may have lived a garden lecturer's fantasy of appearing on television, but not a grown man's fantasy. In the end, I knew that it wasn't Susan Powell or any other Miss America that could ever occupy my day-to-day fantasy world.

Only my wife, Arlene, ably and willingly occupies that post.

And that, thankfully, I know.

Will I Ever Get Out of This Lady's
Bedroom Closet Alive?

I went deeper into the dark recesses of the woman's closet. I had just met her that week and now her garments were draped over me. With my heart hammering, I couldn't help thinking that her husband would burst into the closet, find me, rearrange my face with a few well-placed punches, and throw me out of the upstairs window.

How did I get into this predicament? I simply wanted to take a few photographs for a magazine article about African violets. Now I was facing more humiliation and danger than any garden writer would expect to encounter.

This adventure started when a local African violet aficionado gave a program to my local garden club. The highlight was a plant that was a direct descendent of the native East African violets (*Saintpaulia ionantha*) that were found in 1892 by Baron Walter von Saint Paul. I also learned about hybridized violets whose leaves had a tremendous variety of shapes, sizes, and colors; and flowers that were doubled, frilled, and bicolored.

The seed was planted in my mind at that program. I would do an article about the discovery and hybridization of this one diminutive plant that has had a place in virtually every avid gardener's home. I imagined that the article would practically write itself, since both hybridizers and expert growers were nearby. At the beginning, it seemed like a mythical, journalistic quest, and I imagined myself joining the ranks of Edward R. Murrow, Walter Cronkite, and Woodward and Bernstein.

I got the go-ahead from my editor, Jean Byrne, and began by taking photographs of the winners in the African violet classes at the Philadelphia Flower Show.

The next step was more difficult. I was foolish enough to let my daughter, who was a new driver, take me to the Philadelphia African Violet Society's Flower Show. We got there by way of the Schuylkill (pronounced "sku kill") Expressway and Lincoln Drive. Most people in Philadelphia think Lincoln Drive is the most dangerous road in America. The speed limit is 25 mph, but the average driver goes 45 mph while whipping around curves with rock outcroppings. The Schuylkill Expressway is only slightly less terrifying. In fact, many locals have appropriately renamed it the "Sure Kill Expressway." Amid mutual screams and hysterics, we arrived with her in tears and me in need of a stomach transplant.

Things improved once we were inside. I found that the recreation center used for the show had large windows that cast soft light on the violets, giving me perfect conditions for photography.

Some of the specimens were breathtaking, measuring over 20" across with dozens of blossoms. These plants had gone through a regimen that could only be compared to the training of an Olympic athlete. To grow huge African violets, many experts keep blossoms picked off for most of the year, until 6-8 weeks before the show.

Aside from the huge hybridized plants, there was a display of all of the known *Saintpaulia* species. Some were simply curiosities, but it was the original African violet, *S. ionantha*, that was captivating. Judy Smith, who was the "Species Chairperson" of the club, grew many of these plants. And, at this event, she had won a best-of-show award for a modern hybrid that was 22" across.

I interviewed her for my article, and, even though we had just met, Judy trusted me enough to let me take pictures of the violets in her home. A week later, when I went to her house, I thought her husband would be a commanding presence during the photo shoot, but I found that we were alone. And, where did she grow most of her African violets? In her bedroom, of course.

I took most of the photographs without a hitch. But when I started to run out of film, I had to load a partially used roll. This required a completely dark room to advance the film, but Judy had no such place in her home since there were windows everywhere.

Growing desperate, my eyes alighted on her bedroom closet. When I asked if I could use it, she looked at me in astonishment, but agreed. We took out a few boxes so I could fit inside; then, after wedging myself into a corner, I began advancing the film. While doing so, my mind's eye imaged that her husband was the size of a professional wrestler. He'd come home and find me in his wife's closet, yank me out, assume my camera had indiscreet pictures of his spouse, expose my film, and throw me out of a second floor window. With her clothes enshrouding me, I quickly advanced the film and popped out of the closet like a Jack-in-the-box. Still feeling skittish, I finished my shots and left as soon as I could.

On the way home, in my reverie, I was sure that my horticultural exploits had once again made a rather odd impression on a local gardener.

A week later, I visited Anne and Frank Tinari, a couple who had been in the African violet business since 1945 and were responsible for creating over four hundred new hybrids. The interview and photo session went well, and, before leaving, I purchased a book about African violets.

I wrote the first draft of the article and was about to call the Tinaris to ask them a few more questions, when I received an envelope from them in the mail. I was horrified to find that the check I had used to pay for the African violet book had bounced! Since the Tinaris didn't accept credit cards, I had used an old check in my wallet — regrettably, a check from my bank before it was taken over by another company.

In other words, I had written a bogus check from a nonexistent bank.

I called Anne Tinari and tried to clarify what had happened, but she said, "I understand, this has happened to some of our other customers over the years." Again, I tried to explain, but received the same response. Fortunately, she was warm-hearted enough to answer questions from a check-kiting, would-be reporter.

In the end, the pay I received for writing the article was enough to cover any other bad checks I might have written. But it wouldn't have been enough to pay any medical bills for injuries inflicted by an angry husband who discovered me in his wife's closet. So, I took the safe route: I bought a lightproof bag to change film, and decided to forget about journalistic quests and write about my own horticultural shenanigans for a while.

Q + A = ZZZZZ

Question: "What can I do about the mottled brown spots on the leaves of my *Pleiogynium cerasiferum?*"

Answer: Is anybody out there still awake? Are you still breathing? Or, perhaps you no longer have a detectable pulse.

This is the type of question that many horticultural magazines persist in printing month after month and year after year. Unless the question at hand is the exact one upon which you've been obsessing, you zoom right past the Q&A column to meatier topics — if you aren't already in dreamland.

I have to admit that I've been party to this sedative writing. A few years ago, I assisted a writer from a national gardening magazine who had to answer a question about forcing daffodils. I've no doubt that my contribution was as effective as a tranquilizer gun. The problem, of course, is that most gardening Q&A columns redefine the limits of boredom, and have the collective excitement of a TV test pattern.

To make them more compelling, I suggest that these columns focus on truly important questions from gardeners and their friends and families.

I offer, below, a few modest examples of what could help make the Q&A genre a bit more stimulating.

****

Question: "My wife bought her first cactus on our honeymoon. Since then, I've had to share my home with samples of every spiny plant on the planet. Our vacations are even planned around cactus conventions throughout the world. I reached the limit of my patience last week, when a midnight visit to the bathroom left my posterior scarred and wounded. It turned out that she had put the toilet lid down and was using it to hold some newly purchased cacti. What can I do?"

Answer: Obviously, her cacti have taken over your house and are ruling your life. It's time to put your foot down. The only solution is to keep a bedpan close at hand, and be sure to check the floor for spiny specimens before you put down that foot of yours.

♦♦♦♦♦♦♦♦

Question: "We're in debt and are about to be evicted from our house because of the money my husband spends on bulbs every year. He forces them into bloom for our midwinter flower show, and the blue ribbons he wins are more important to him than having a roof over our heads. We have no choice but to leave our lovely home and move to a one-bedroom apartment. Can you give me some advice?"

Answer: My wife and I have had similar conversations, so you've asked the right person. My advice is to get an apartment with a southern exposure. Also, be sure to set the thermostat no higher than 65°F, otherwise your husband's bulbs won't bloom properly.

♦♦♦♦♦♦♦♦

Question: "African violets entrance my wife, Paula. I didn't used to mind it so much, but things have become desperate. She's been missing for three days, and yesterday I found a receipt from our travel agent for $1,657. I called the agent and learned that Paula used the money for a trip to Kenya — where African violets grow in the wild. To make matters worse, I'm the treasurer of our garden club, and today I discovered that exactly $1,657 is missing from the club's account. I'm certain that my wife is the culprit. Can you help me?"

Answer: This is a terrible scandal that, if left unsolved, could limit your horticultural activities to prison gardening. Fortunately, you've written to the appropriate garden writer for advice, since I've helped other clubs expose fiscal improprieties. To conduct a thorough investigation, I'll need a blank check from your club's account and the name of your wife's travel agent. It may take me a while to complete my research; but, if I happen to see your wife in Africa, we'll be sure to send you dried African violet flowers and a picture postcard from Kenya. I don't know if or when we'll be back, but at least you'll have two souvenirs to prove to club members that their money was spent appropriately.

Question: "Two weeks ago, a library volunteer thought she saw someone cutting off marigold blossoms in our Storytime Garden. We went outside to investigate and found that twenty blossoms were missing. What's especially galling is that the perpetrator did this within eyesight of the police station that sits next to the library. Then, last week, the incriminating evidence was there for everyone to see: Our suspect entered a flower arrangement in the local garden show, and it contained twenty marigolds of exactly the same cultivar as those in our Storytime Garden. What can I do to put an end to this?"

Answer: I think the only solution is to drop a trail of marigolds every fifty feet between the garden and the nearby jail. Be sure to put some flower arranging tools and a vase in the jail cell, and close the door with a decided clang as soon as she's taken the "bait."

♦♦♦♦♦♦♦♦

Question: "My wife is upset because I grow my orchids on the dining room table. She's also indignant because I took down our chandelier and replaced it with grow lamps. Now she's furious because I set up a humidifier next to the table. What can I do to save my orchids from her wrath?"

Answer: It sounds as if you've done almost everything right so far, but orchids don't need a humidifier quite so close. I would take the china out of your breakfront, leave the doors open, and place the humidifier inside.

♦♦♦♦♦♦♦♦

Question: "A new family with teenage boys moved in next door. Last week they installed a basketball court in their backyard. Now their kids are climbing our fence to retrieve basketballs. They're not only destroying the fence, but my vegetable garden. What can I do?"

Answer: There's a new company called Hidden Shock that electrifies fences without using wires. After one zap, you won't have to worry about teenagers climbing your fence. The basketballs will probably continue landing in your yard, but you can cut them in half and use them to cover seedlings for protection from springtime frosts.

Question: "Because of a dry spring, we have drought restrictions in my area. As a result, I haven't been able to water my flower garden in over a month and it looks awful. What can I do?"

Answer: Seal off the drain in your bathtub and put soup pots on the bathroom floor. Next, make sure your family only takes showers in the evening. After they're finished, have them use the pots to scoop out the dirty water and use it on your plants when your neighbors aren't watching. I have two more suggestions: Buy everyone in your family a few pairs of long black sox to hide the bathtub scum on their feet. And, when you make soup in the pots next winter, triple the usual amount of spices.

♦♦♦♦♦♦♦♦

Question: "During the Philadelphia Flower Show every March, I always buy more plants than I can fit in my car. Should I stop attending?"

Answer: Of course not. It's obviously time to get your fellow garden club members involved. Buy everyone tickets to the show, with the understanding that you'll use every bit of space in their cars for your new plants. It may be more expensive than renting a moving van, but your fellow club members will be able to use their car heaters to keep your plants warm. Just be sure to leave a gap between the foliage so the driver can see out of the front window. After all, you want your plants to arrive alive.

****

Well, I hope you've enjoyed my version of a livelier Q&A column. On the other hand, you may be the only one that's made it this far — meaning I've been every bit as successful as a traditional Q&A columnist in sending readers to the land of Wynken, Blynken, and Nod.

Although I can delude myself into thinking that I've improved an old literary art form, perhaps like dogs, it may be best to let sleeping Q&A columns lie — asleep and unpublished.

Better Bulbs and Blossoms

I had only one large pot of tulips for a *Better Homes and Gardens* (*BH&G*) photography session; and here it was, three mornings before the shoot, and each blossom was frozen solid, looking like contorted peach popsicles. I had misjudged the weather, ruined the shoot, and wasted six months of hard work. The contingent from *BH&G* — including an executive garden editor, an art editor, a photographer, a photographer's assistant, a stylist, and a stylist's assistant — was poised to produce two magazine articles about how to force bulbs. But this disaster necessitated a rethinking of the articles: Art Wolk was going to show the world how *not* to force bulbs.

****

This saga began when I took a photography workshop in September 1998 at Longwood Gardens. It was a marvelous one-day class taught by Mark Kane, a garden editor from *BH&G*. When the class ended, I summoned a bit of courage and asked for Kane's business card, thinking I might call him to discuss an idea for a magazine article.

Before I contacted Kane, I thought about the fact that there are magazines, Magazines, and MAGAZINES, and that *BH&G* is definitely in the latter category. It has the highest circulation of any garden periodical in the United States, which translates into a higher fee being paid and, just as importantly, the widest national exposure.

These thoughts danced in my head while I considered what type of article I would suggest to Kane. But after choosing a topic, I felt intimidated.

October passed.

November passed.

And December was about to end.

Finally, with my notes in hand, I took a deep breath, picked up the receiver, and called *BH&G* headquarters in Des Moines, Iowa. It was exactly like my teenage years, when I had to work up enough nerve to call a girl for a date. Back then, I'd dial the phone number and, feeling a bit queasy, actually hope no one was home. Or worse, if someone picked up the phone, I was just as likely to hang up as I was to stammer a greeting.

After one ring, I heard, "Hello, Mark Kane." In an instant, his affable, unassuming nature put me at ease, and we began talking to one another like old friends.

When I suggested that we work together on an article about bulb forcing, I heard frustration in his voice.

"We've been trying to do an article about that for three years and have failed each time," he said.

I mentioned the experience I had gained after two decades of exhibiting at the Philadelphia Flower Show, and he immediately sounded interested. Kane said that my timing was perfect, because by early February 1999 he had to tell his boss about every gardening article that would be in the 2000 *BH&G* issues.

Next, we began to put together an outline for the piece. It would be done in three parts:

- The first would involve pots filled with only one kind of bulb.
- The second would show readers how to produce a bulb-garden pot, in which a variety of bulbs would be planted together. During midwinter indoor forcing, this pot would create a sequence of blooms, simulating an outdoor spring.
- The third part would involve forcing a variety of bulbs (e.g., *Iris reticulata, Crocus*, tulips, daffodils, and grape hyacinths) to bloom simultaneously, then arranging them in a "bouquet" pot.

Kane said that the breadth of bulb forcing we discussed would probably culminate in two articles being published in the October 2000 issue. Our conversation went more smoothly than I could have ever expected. The only catch was determining exactly where we would do the fall and mid-winter photo shoots.

Kane informed me that only *BH&G* editors write articles, but that my pay would be significant for serving as the grower and expert. At the end of our conversation he asked me to send him photos of a variety of rooms in my house, so the *BH&G* Art Department could decide if our home was appropriate for indoor photography.

I very slowly replaced the receiver with a twin sense of elation and dread. I was thrilled over the possibility of doing articles for a magazine with a circulation of seven million, but felt anxious about telling my wife that our home might be used for the photo shoot.

I approached the topic delicately, saying, "Hey honey, I'm going to be doing an article about bulb forcing."

"That's nice dear; for which magazine?"

"It's really going to help my horticultural career."

"So which magazine is it?" she persisted.

"It's got a circulation of seven million, hon."

She narrowed her eyes and said, "*Why aren't you telling me?*"

"Oh alright, it's *Better Homes and Gardens*. And they'll probably take a few photos in our house," I barely murmured.

Lowering the volume didn't work; she heard every vowel and consonant. "You're kidding, right? You don't think for a moment that they're coming to this house, do you?"

"Actually, they'll do most of the photography outside and in the greenhouse, sweetie."

She didn't buy it for a second.

"You can forget it! Your potted bulbs would make a mess that would be traipsed all over the house."

I had to admit that she was right. Our house was a shambles the years I had won the Philadelphia Flower Show Grand Sweepstakes Award, and I was going to do just as much bulb forcing for the *BH&G* articles. In the end, I never sent them a single picture of our home or garden.

So, I began my quest to find homeowners willing to have their homes turned into a jumble of cargo, cables, and cameras.

The shoots would take place in the fall of 1999, when the bulbs would be planted, and late winter of 2000, when the flowering bulbs would be at their peak.

It didn't take long to find out that most people had a very different view of a *BH&G* photo shoot from my wife. Arlene would have been ready to commit spousal homicide if I let anyone from *BH&G* within zoom lens range of our house. But there were plenty of homeowners who would commit homicide if anyone tried to keep a *BH&G* photographer away from their homes, since it would give them bragging rights and notoriety.

Once gossip spread about my *BH&G* article, I became the "flavor of the month" in Southern New Jersey. Friends, non-friends, and a few outright enemies vied for the exalted status of a *BH&G* homeowner. I spent two days taking photos of the exteriors of suburban homes for the outdoor shoot and sent them to Mark Kane and the photographer, Allison Miksch.

Eventually, they decided which home to use and set a date for early November 1999.

On the appointed day, the photographer, her assistant, and Arlene and I gathered bulbs, pots, flats,* soil, labels, and camera gear in the backyard of my friend, Judy Gates. At that point, I'd written and taken photos for sixteen magazine articles, but it didn't prepare me for a *BH&G* photography session.

Here's what was photographed:

- me potting one type of bulb in a 10" pot,
- me potting one type of bulb in a flat,
- me potting a mixture of bulbs in a 12" pot,
- me carrying a pot, and
- me burying a pot in the ground.

Sounds quick and simple, right? Actually, it was long and complicated.

Miksch snapped about six hundred shots between 10:00 AM and sunset. Of those six hundred, exactly two photographs made it into the articles.

Once the first shoot was completed, one would have thought that my work was half finished, but it was just beginning: I had $500 worth of bulbs to plant in preparation for the late February shoot. So, every

---

*A flat is a container 1' long by 2' wide by 3" deep that has a plastic insert with 18–48 openings in which plants can be grown.

day for two weeks, I filled flats and dozens of pots, including five bulb-garden pots, with bulbs.*

After all the bulbs were planted, they were tucked into my two thermostatically-controlled cold frames.

Next, I searched for homes for the February shoot, and once again, numerous homeowners vied for the exalted status that a *BH&G* article would provide. Arlene lined up six homes in historic Moorestown, New Jersey, where I took wide-angle photos. Some of the homes were glorious Victorians with lavish wood paneling and sunrooms bigger than an average living room. Eventually, three of them were anointed the sites for the February photographs.

When the shoot was five weeks away, I brought flats, pots of tulips, and the first bulb-garden pot into my greenhouse. With four weeks to go, more tulips and another bulb-garden pot were brought inside. And three weeks before the shoot, daffodils, hyacinths, and the third bulb-garden pot came in.

Even with twenty-five years of bulb forcing experience, it's always at this stage that things can get scary. The tulips had been inside for two weeks, but seemed to be in suspended animation. They had gone from very small green pips of growth to what looked like even smaller pips of growth.

With three weeks to go, everything seemed behind schedule. I had a horrible feeling that my flowers wouldn't be ready until a week after the pre-arranged dates for photography.

In a panic, I asked various members of the *BH&G* team if we could delay the shoot by a week. The consensus was a definite no. Almost everyone had other assignments before and after the designated two days in February.

I swallowed hard and realized that doing the photography on February 25th and 26th was a do-or-die situation. I felt more pressure

---

*Since the photo shoot was to take place on two successive days in February, I had to plant five 12" bulb-garden pots. Each pot was the same size and contained the same types of bulbs in the same quantities and positions. One bulb-garden pot was brought into my greenhouse once a week for the five weeks preceding the shoot. On the day they were photographed, the five pots showed indoor forcing after 1, 2, 3, 4, and 5 weeks. This enabled us to show the reader the sequence of blooms (i.e., *Crocus*, then grape hyacinths, then daffodils and hyacinths, and finally tulips) that they could expect if they used just one bulb-garden pot.

than the first year I tried to win the Philadelphia Flower Show's Grand Sweepstakes. If I had failed in my quest for that award, I would have been the only person inconvenienced. This was a very different situation.

Not only were the people immediately involved in producing the magazine articles depending on my capabilities, but there were undoubtedly dozens of other people behind-the-scenes who expected these two articles to appear in the October 2000 issue.

Fortunately, my bulbs began to grow faster — in fact, too fast. I went from the terrible fear that nothing would bloom in time to the dread that everything would peak too soon.

With two weeks to go, the weather outside warmed to spring-like temperatures and every one of my flower buds started to show color. My guardian angel was Nancy, the local convenience store manager, who let me use her walk-in refrigerator to hold back my bulbs. The only problem was the volume of space I needed for six 12" pots, six 10" pots, a dozen 6" pots, and ten 2' X 1' flats.

Although it was wonderful having the resource of a walk-in refrigerator, space was limited, and accidents could occur. I was especially concerned about my largest pot of tulips: lovely peach-colored flowers named 'Apricot Beauty.' Four days before the shoot they were perfect, so holding them back would take some creativity. I was afraid to take them to the convenience store's walk-in refrigerator, but I still had my cold frames and the weather forecast on my side. The night of February 21st was supposed to stay above freezing, so I put the tulips in my cold frame and went to bed confident that I had everything under control.

The next morning, I snuck a peak out the window and saw what looked like a landscape that had been painted with a frost-colored brush. The lawn, shed, and cold frames were covered with it.

Startled, I threw clothes over my pajamas, then ran to the frame that held my tulips. Raising the window, I saw the hideous sight of arthritic peach tulips whose every petal, leaf, and stem was frozen and bent over. Twelve hours earlier these tulips were going to be the stars of the *BH&G* photo shoot. Now, they were ready to be fallen stars on my compost heap.

I was devastated and inconsolable.

With the care normally reserved for newborns, I lifted the pot out of the cold frame and carefully placed it in a sunny area of my back-yard. I had a tiny hope that this treatment would revive the tulips.

At work, I couldn't help but think about the shoot I had probably ruined, since no other tulip pots were this big or colorful. At lunchtime, I raced home from work, threw open the garden gate, and ran to my tulips. Miraculously, they had transformed back into the perfect, straight-stemmed specimens of the night before. Thanks to the warm, gentle sun, the photo shoot had been saved.

For the next two days, I worked frantically to push bulbs ahead or hold them back. And, my efforts paid off: On the night before the photo shoot, I loaded a rented van with pots and flats that held flowering bulbs at their peak. I stared at the mass of flowers and relaxed. They looked gorgeous.

I awoke the next morning to an outdoor world that had become spring overnight. There were sunny skies and temperatures over 60°F, meaning I would have to work hard to keep my blooms from droop-ing. Fortunately, when I arrived at the first home for our shoot, I found that they had a large, shaded porch. It was the perfect place to cool my flowers.

Once everything was out of the van, I fell into a soft chair on the porch. Surveying my blooming bulbs, I felt true satisfaction: I had deliv-ered what was expected of me.

But I deluded myself into thinking that I wouldn't have much work left to do. All day long I had to lug heavy pots up and down steep stairs. To make matters worse, the temperatures on the second and third floors were too warm for my flowers. So I took pots upstairs long enough for a preliminary set-up, then returned them to the cool porch. When everything else in the room was arranged and they were ready to snap photographs, I'd take the same pots back upstairs.

The scenes weren't created without guidelines. We had received photographic directions from Kane, who was back in Des Moines. It was up to Ted Rossiter, *BH&G*'s senior graphic designer, and Alison Miksch to decide which rooms they would use to fulfill Kane's requests. It was fascinating to watch them in action; they were both like dessert connoisseurs in a bakery, with a new pastry around every corner. As they passed from one space to another, they mentally kept track of which shots they would take. For me, this was nothing less than a college course in how a high-circulation magazine produces articles.

In addition to Ted, Alison, and me, our team also included Barbara Fritz, who was a stylist. Say the word "stylist" to most people, and they'll think of a hairstylist, but Barbara was anything but that. She had a truckload of curios, props, flowerpot holders, and other materials that were used to produce the desired mood.

Ted, Alison, and Barbara took their time to carefully set up each scene. As I surveyed the view in front of the camera, I realized that many of Barbara's props were present. In fact, I can't remember a single shot during those two days that involved only my flowers and the homeowners' décor and furniture.

Once a room was prepared for photography, a Polaroid (instantly developed) shot was taken. Next, adjustments of the props, flowers, furniture, and lighting were made until Ted was happy with the results; then Alison started using large quantities of high-quality (Provia 100) film. Ultimately, for every picture published in the magazine, at least one hundred photographs were taken.

At that point in my life, I was reading books on artistic composition to become a better photographer. So, as each scene was set up, I could see the principles and elements of composition that were being used to create photos.

For one magical photograph, I was asked to wash every bit of soil from three pots of *Iris reticulata* — a process that seemed to take forever.

When I was finished, I stuffed the irises into parfait glasses and Ted and Alison arranged them on a windowsill. Next, the window was sprayed with water, so it would appear to be a rainy day. Once everything was arranged, I understood the mood they were trying to achieve. The roots, now showing through the glasses, matched the white window treatment, and the blue *Iris* blossoms were the perfect accent for the watery window and prevailing white.

The picture told a story: You've just awakened, rolled over, and looked at the windowsill holding the irises. It was a dreary winter day outside, but the flowers put a smile on your face. You had jumped ahead to spring and it was right there inside your window.

We all agreed that this would probably be the best shot of all. It was sheer elegance.

As the sun got close to the horizon, that day's photography was about to end. Suddenly, I realized that they hadn't taken pictures of the five 12" pots that showed the spring-like progression of blossoming bulbs. So I got everyone's attention, and we hurried outside to use the last bit of daylight. Although five different pots were photographed, in the magazine article it appeared as if the same pot was photographed once a week, over a five-week period.

One day down, one day to go.

I was worn out, but packed every pot and flat into my rented van. Luckily, the weather forecast predicted temperatures above 40°F, so I left everything in place: safe, secure, and protected.

The next morning, we arrived at the second Victorian home twenty minutes before dawn. It was misty outside, but it was the exact atmosphere they wanted.

Alison took photographs of a pot of hyacinths placed next to a decrepit pergola that was going to be replaced that summer. The homeowners thought it was more than a little ironic that the main shots at their property would be of a tottering pergola. They had a sumptuous sunroom inside, but it was so big that using it would have required more props and time than we had on this last day of shooting.

When we arrived at the final site for photography, we found the family buzzing with excitement. The husband wanted to record the day's events, so he took pictures of the photographer taking pictures. He said that if any of his friends doubted that a *BH&G* photo session had occurred at their house, he would have proof to show them what had transpired.

Actually, what transpired was nothing short of legerdemain. After a quick survey of the home by Alison and Ted, they started to ignore what pieces of furniture were in each room or their weight. The tables, plates, and keepsakes became the oils they would use to "paint" photographs. Within thirty minutes, the dining room table, which was a converted barn door, was taken into the middle of the living room.

Barbara elegantly decorated the table using her props, while I made three centerpieces in metal chalices using crocuses, miniature daffodils, and white tulips. To complete the setting, pears and a wine bottle were added.

This sounds like the sham of the century, but it worked. The blue dining room table matched the blue wall coverings in the living room. The yellow in the crocuses and daffodils was complementary to the blue, and the white tulips matched the white window treatments. Again, Alison and Ted had used great imagination to orchestrate a marvelous photograph.

Next, we moved the barn door dining room table into a sunroom. Here, a huge 12" pot of grape hyacinths blended with the table; white tulips were in harmony with the white window frames; and yellow daffodils were complementary to the grape hyacinths, making them both more striking.

By the time the shoot was over, I came to believe that not a single article in high-circulation interior design magazines contains only the owner's décor. And, even if the owners' décor is used, some if not all of it is shifted before the photos are taken. The artistic team on our photo shoot simply knew how to create the best pictures a house could provide. It was exactly what I had learned from artistic composition books: Painters may have a scene in front of them, but they add or subtract elements to produce a good composition.

As the day came to a close, I remembered Kane's photo order, especially the picture that was supposed to include me. I mentioned this to Alison and Ted, and they immediately stopped what they were doing. We quickly went to the porch and set up a table where I began potting daffodils. Ted got me to look up by chatting with me so that Alison could get a good shot. My extroverted nature got in the way, but Alison managed to capture a photo when I was smiling instead of talking.

The shoot was finished, and I started gathering my supplies. Ted suggested that I give a few of my potted bulbs to the homeowners, and I agreed. In addition, other people from the crew wanted some of my flowers. At first I felt like a father giving up his children, but another feeling was even stronger: Everyone was complimenting my capabilities by coveting my bulbs. In the end, I realized that giving away my flowers was the best way I could thank them.

Seven months later, just before the October 2000 issue of *BH&G* was published, Kane told me that a lot of people would fall in love with me after reading the articles. That struck me as rather odd; I thought he was exaggerating.

He wasn't.

When the October 2000 *BH&G* came out, so did the lovefest. People I hadn't seen or spoken to for years called or wrote letters to me. My father, who showed real pride, told me about every single one of his visits to doctors' offices over the next four months. Each waiting room had the issue and he made sure everybody in the office saw it. It was all very heady, but a bit strange. Some of my friends started to treat me differently, as if I were something akin to nobility. I felt proud of my accomplishment, but wanted to be treated the same as always.

On the other hand, my wife and daughter may have shown just as much pride as my father, but they were extremely good at keeping me grounded in reality. The day the articles first appeared, there was one thing that didn't change at all: Just like the other 364 days of the year, Art Wolk took out the garbage.

"Johnny has very low horticultural aptitude...
he may have to become a doctor or a lawyer."

10

DID YOU EVER
THINK ABOUT ...?

What It Would Be Like
If Everyone Were a Gardener

IT'S FRUSTRATING TRYING TO MAKE non-gardening friends, neighbors, and family members understand the mindset of a gardener. We can't fathom why non-gardeners go into a rage about the dirt, expense, and our single-minded obsessiveness. Nor do we understand why they don't enjoy tilling the earth, watching a seed germinate, or coaxing a plant to bloom.

We can't help but dream of a world composed of only gardeners — with people in sympathy with our frustrations, fears, hopes, and moments of elation. At first thought, it would seem to be a planet filled with beauty, camaraderie, and domestic tranquility. But, after a bit more contemplation, I believe it wouldn't be quite the worldwide flower garden first envisioned.

So before any of us runs off to rub Aladdin's lamp, perhaps we should pause to contemplate the consequences of a world filled with people of our ilk.

Here's what I think such a place would be like:

- Since no real gardener ever moves to an area with a shorter outdoor growing season, everyone on earth eventually would be clustered within 500 miles of the equator.
- Children who show no aptitude or interest in gardening would be sent to special education classes and evaluated by the school physician for the best course of drug and psychological therapy. If their condition couldn't be corrected, the child would be recommended for the lowly callings of doctor or lawyer.

- Flower shows would become international events — similar to a current-day Olympics — with tickets gobbled up a decade in advance. Entire Flower Show Villages would be built, and an International Flower Show Committee would select the site of each year's extravaganza. TV coverage would be beamed to every home and school, and the most anticipated event would be the selection of gold, silver, and bronze winners in each horticultural class. Multiple gold medal winners would be given lucrative contracts to have their picture on boxes of "Wheaties — The Breakfast of Champions!"
- Although trash collectors would no longer have to pick up curbside leaves, neighbors would fight over each leaf needed to fatten their compost piles.
- The athletic Olympics would have a complete overhaul of sporting events. Swimming races would be dropped in favor of water garden construction races; the 4 X 100 yard relay would hand off a lawn mower instead of a baton; and archery events would use photos of offensive garden pests as targets instead of standard bull's-eyes.
- Following the laws of supply and demand, the seeds of each new hybrid would have an astronomical price and would be delivered to wealthy gardeners in a Brink's truck.
- The world's supply of peat moss would be depleted in two generations, so everyone would use compost-based mixes that they pasteurize in their ovens.
- Garden supply centers would have more security guards than the local bank, and a picture ID would be needed to gain entrance. Security devices at the exit would detect anything containing chlorophyll that hadn't been desensitized at the cash register.
- Stealing a cutting would be considered a felony and the premeditated killing of a plant would be a capital offense.
- Garden clubs would be so numerous that public meeting places would be booked twenty years in advance.
- The major political parties would be the Organics and Inorganics, with each one having to court the favor of the Hydroponics, Topiaries, and Indoor Gardeners to form a coalition government.

- A law promoting the eradication of rabbits, groundhogs, deer, moles, and other garden pests would win unanimous approval in the U.S. House and Senate. These animals would be placed at the top of a newly created "Pursued Species List."
- The work year would run from the first autumnal frost until the last spring frost. The workweek wouldn't run from Monday to Friday, but from the beginning to the end of a lightning storm that halts garden activity.
- Horticultural Schools would have the toughest entry requirements, with high Horticultural Achievement Test scores being an important prerequisite for admission.
- Las Vegas hotels would drop their glitzy shows. In their place, the most entertaining garden lecturers would be booked years in advance, with tickets sold for at least half a week's salary.
- Communities would have fines imposed for neighbors having more than 40% of their yard composed of lawn grass. Jail sentences would be imposed for residents with any compostable matter found in their trash.
- Farmers wouldn't worry about the market price of tomatoes per pound, since everybody would grow their own tomatoes. The main topic of conversation among farmers would be the price of cow manure per pound.
- The most expensive cars would be those that have the greatest capacity for hauling manure, so the Cadillac El Dorado would go out of production in favor of the high-capacity Cadillac Hearse.
- The only outdoor "pets" would be dried manure pet sculptures. Indoor pets would go to schools for plant-aversion training.
- During the winter, the highest percentage of everyone's household budget would be spent on cut flowers. Given this demand, the price of a dozen roses would soar to $200.

After reviewing this list, I think we might be better off having our share of non-gardening friends and neighbors. We'll still get stared at as if we're ready for the loony bin, but at least we'll have people to pity every time we step into our gardens. And besides, wouldn't our world be terribly diminished if we couldn't watch the neck veins of neighboring non-gardeners swell when we get rid of the front lawn to create a flower or vegetable garden?

The Most Dangerous Hobby of All: Gardening

The pulse races, the stomach churns, and the eyes bulge for those brave people who spend their weekends hang gliding, bungee jumping, or downhill skiing. More sedate people can't understand what drives others to engage in such dangerous enterprises. They think, *Why don't those insane people stay around home and find a safe and serene hobby like gardening?*

But what the naysayers don't realize is that although "home is where the heart is," it's also where danger lies lurking. Think about it: Aside from your car, where have most of your accidents occurred? Unless you're a fraudulent faller, it's right at home.

This issue begs the question of what the most dangerous home activity happens to be, and it doesn't take a university professor to figure out that it's gardening.

Tell me if I'm wrong, but don't gardeners use or come in contact with poison ivy, poison sumac, bees, wasps, spiders, insecticides, herbicides, fungicides, tall ladders, lawn mowers, mulchers, power saws, rototillers, axes, pitchforks, and knives? Although many of these items sound like the materiel in the haversacks of World War I soldiers, they are only a partial list of the dangerous flora, fauna, tools, and chemicals with which an average gardener comes into contact.

You may think my list is overwrought, but I've had first-hand experience with many of these hazards. Let me describe just one example: When I was twenty-one years old, I was stung on the tip of my little finger by a bee. Within ten minutes, I could hardly breathe and was losing consciousness. Luckily, I was around the corner from a hospital, where I came very close to bidding farewell to life. The next day, the chief resident told me that if I had arrived five minutes later, I would have been dead on arrival.

So, now I have to carry a hypodermic syringe filled with adrenaline wherever I go. And what hobby have I chosen? Life-threatening gardening, of course. I promised my wife, Arlene, that if she married me, she'd never be bored. But I think she'd appreciate a big dose of "boring" whenever she drives me to an emergency room after I've been stung in the garden.

At this point, you're probably thinking, *Well, garden bugs may be dangerous for Art Wolk, but not for me.* And, all I can say is, what closet have you been hiding in?

Wherever you live in the United States there are probably disease-carrying ticks waiting to dine on your blood. And, since the early 1980s, the Northeast Coastal Region and the Midwest has become infested with the deer tick that transmits Lyme disease — an insidious ailment that causes malaise at best and meningitis and palsy at worst.* It would be hard enough to identify the offending critter if it were the same size as a dog tick, but it's approximately three-times smaller, or the size of a pinhead.

One of my friends has figured out an interesting method of dealing with this tick. She lives in woods infested with them, so she dons a unique outfit when she dares to garden. There are white tennis shoes on her feet, and inside the tennis shoes are white socks into which she tucks white sweat pants. Of course, she also wears a white sweatshirt that she tucks into her pants. A white scarf covers her hair and a white garden hat covers the scarf. Finally, white garden gloves finish off this tick-induced fashion statement.

By wearing this outfit, my friend can spot a tick in seconds. But her scheme prompts two questions: First, does she ever have time to garden, or does she spend the entire day keeping both eyes peeled for pepper-sized ticks? Second, how can she stand the glare reflected by her outfit? Perhaps she not only needs sunglasses, but a sunblock lotion of SPF1000 when she gardens.

Delving a bit further into the subject of sunblock, scientists tell us that we can no longer frolic in our gardens on sunny days without lathering up every two hours — unless we don't care about the skin cancer

---

*Other ticks that transmit Lyme Disease are the western black-legged tick in the South and the lone star tick in the West.

that our hobby might cause. So to protect ourselves against both ticks and sunlight, we wear an outfit like my friend's as well as very wide-brimmed, sun-blocking hats that make us look like we're wearing an umbrella. Upon reflection, I've little doubt that dangerous sun rays will eventually make subterranean mushroom gardening the wave of the future.

Aside from life-threatening insects and sunshine, other dangers lurk along the primrose path.

Another friend of mine is an avid gardener whose garden-related allergy takes a different form from mine. In her case, poison ivy is the culprit. I'm sure you're saying to yourself that virtually everyone is allergic to poison ivy, but the lady in question redefines the limits of sensitivity.

Her worst reaction occurred after she drove her car past a field where poison ivy was being cut. Within a few hours she broke out into red welts and eventually missed a week of work. Naturally, she headed outside as soon as she recovered and had another reaction to the stuff lurking in her own backyard.

Sometimes the sun, ticks, or poisonous plants aren't the problem. I have one friend in Virginia who was actually attacked by her garden. She was on a ladder pruning a tree, when one of the cut branches swung around and knocked her to the ground. Her injuries were so severe that it took six months for her to recover. What surprises me most is that she's still gardening at all.

Then there are the tools, or should I say arsenal, of our hobby. Is there an avid gardener anywhere who hasn't had a self-inflicted wound resulting from the inaccurate use of a shovel, trowel, ax, knife, pruning shears, or pitchfork?

I can remember one hot, exhausting day when I thrust a shovel toward the ground, but hit my foot instead. If it weren't for my Wellie boots, I'd now only have to take care of six toes, not ten.

Although manual tools can be dangerous, it's the self-powered tools that are the real "Backyard Robocops." Each electric- or gas-powered garden tool comes with an instruction book that is complicated at best and inaccurate at worst. And, let's face it, when you're a weekend gardener with limited time, are you really going to take the six hours needed to read every word in these terrible tomes?

So off you go with your new power saw, power trimmer, power mower, or power edger, all of which are capable of removing one or more of your digits. I could describe each worst-case scenario, but perhaps it's best that I don't go into the gory possibilities. Suffice it to say that I wish I could tell you that none of my acquaintances have lost a body part using these tools, but I can't.

So the next time you prepare to go into your backyard to plant a few petunias, perhaps you'd better think twice. After all, there must be a safer way to spend your free time.

Skydiving anyone?

High-Status Gardening

"Who owns the tan minivan? Who owns the tan minivan? Your van is about to be towed!"

Again and again the question is blared inside a health spa, until a very humiliated man admits that he's the owner.

The next televised scene shows a more self-assured man in a sporty convertible with a ravishing woman at his side. Finally, it dawns on me that I'm watching a car commercial that promises to alter my self-image, make me more popular, and change my life from the dull humdrum of being a boring, tan minivan driver.

I have to admit that the notion that certain cars can give you more self-respect and higher status leaves me baffled. When exactly did cars go from being modes of transportation to modes of personality transformation? Aren't cars like shoes, bicycles, rowboats, trains, and jets that simply get you from point A to point B? Don't get me wrong, I don't think that airline commercials are so much better that I'd want to spend an afternoon watching them, but at least they're still about getting you to your destination at the lowest cost. And, they haven't started to sell you "image" like car commercials.

This subject begs comparison with the field of horticulture, where status and image reign supreme. When I first started gardening, I thought that the primary aim of a flower gardener was to produce beauty, just like an artist who creates a landscape painting. So I assumed that the focus wasn't on which plants were used, but the overall effect. Gardeners step back, view an entire garden, and feel as if they've been transported to paradise.

But that really isn't the case, is it? There's a very strong horticultural movement afoot that defines which colors are beautiful (usually pastels), which ones aren't (the primaries), which plants should reside in your garden (rare, expensive, difficult-to-grow perennials), and which ones shouldn't (easily grown, inexpensive, common annuals).

Consider a moment: Have you ever heard of a prominent garden society offering a lecture on marigolds, zinnias, or petunias? On the other hand, you certainly see lectures advertised on growing disease-prone roses in regions where they're most susceptible to disease, as well as programs on the intense effort it takes to grow humidity- and heat-hating alpine perennials in very warm, humid regions. These lectures usually last for two hours, and for good reason — it takes that long to learn how to pull these plants back from the brink of death. To the contrary, easy-to-grow annuals not only flourish their first year, but drop seeds and come back year after year, cropping up in pavement cracks, lawns, and fallow garden areas. It's a de facto rule that the very vigor of these annuals makes them horticultural pariahs.

Do you garden with annuals that survive without a botanical first-aid kit? Do they thrive in spite of your absence during summer vacations? Do they naturalize in your backyard without a violent alteration of your garden's environment? Can they be bought without making a significant dent in your checking account? If the answer is yes to any of these questions, then there's rarely a lecture or article about these plants in horticultural halls of prestige or their periodicals.

If you think I'm exaggerating, let me tell you a true story: Not too long ago, I approached a very prestigious horticultural organization on the East Coast about giving a program on economical gardening. The program coordinator laughed and said, "Oh, that would never go over with our audience." It was one of those rare occasions when I was speechless. Upon reflection, I realized that her subtext was, "My clientele only believe in gardening extravagantly, even if it's a total failure."

That conversation left me with questions about her clientele, specifically: Do they grow flowering plants to create a glorious garden scene, or to take pride in the fact that they can keep rare, expensive plants alive in their botanical intensive care unit (ICU)? Do they ever step back and look at their garden as a whole, or do they view their gardens like the second hand on a digital watch — in discrete, individual, blips? The latter has been most accurately described as the "Tweed Bottom" school of garden design, so named for gardeners who wear tweed pants or skirts when they go on garden tours. As they stop at each individual plant, they bend at the waist, show the world their "tweed bottom," and never move back far enough to see the overall garden design. And it's a good thing they don't, because gardens that are merely collections of high-status, high-cost plants redefine the word jumble.

Aside from the joy of managing to keep ICU plants alive from week-to-week, there is, above all else, the aspect of status. Some gardeners are seduced into thinking it would be wonderful to be the first person in their community to own a $300 dwarf pink butterfly bush or a $125 *Iris* with variegated foliage and multicolored blossoms.

To be honest, it's easy to succumb to the temptations of high-status gardening, especially in the winter when we receive catalogs that have such alluring pictures of ICU plants. But, unfortunately, many are unsuited to your environment or your billfold.

So be forewarned: If you surrender your time, garden, and wallet to become a high-status gardener, don't ever (1) take a revealing wide-angle picture of your plant collection, or (2) look over the fence at the low-status plants of your neighbors.

The next-door neighbors may not care about status, but they've somehow managed to produce a lovely garden consisting of marigolds, impatiens, petunias, zinnias, and low-cost native trees, shrubs, and perennials. And by August, you won't see your neighbors at all, because they'll have enough money left in their bank account to go on a vacation across the country ... in a low-status tan minivan.

The Turning-Our-Backs-On-Nature Movement

I'm a baby boomer who attended college during the turbulent 1960s. When I speak to other members of my generation, I've found that many of them look back on those times as if they were utopian. Although the moon landing, Motown, and marches were highlights, I believe they're seeing things through very tinted glasses. Have they forgotten the missiles of October, the three assassinations, the lynchings in the South, the riots in the North, and the war that built a wall between two generations? With all the national angst we were experiencing, many of us longed for the simplicity of our past agrarian society.

It was about that time when we started to pay attention to the new science called ecology, especially after the warnings in Rachel Carlson's *Silent Spring* were shown to have merit. As a result, the back-to-nature movement and organic gardening jolted into prominence. It consisted not only of the flower children of the sixties, but the victory gardeners from World War II. The Rodale "Empire" rode the wave to publishing glory, and *Organic Gardening Magazine* became one of the most popular garden periodicals in the world. By the end of the 1970s, I was also part of the back-to-nature movement and began gardening organically. Since then, I've witnessed the interest in gardening in the United States grow with each passing year.

However, in the 1990s I started to notice another movement growing. But perhaps "growing" is the wrong word. Instead, I should say "being mass-produced." Go into any craft store and you'll know exactly what I'm talking about: Approximately 25% of the floor space is filled with plastic and silk plant imitations. And, with each passing year, more restaurants, office buildings, and homes have plants and trees, indoors and outdoors, made from these materials.

It's what I call the "turning-our-backs-on-nature" movement.

Before this "gardening" revolution took place, I didn't think there was anything "related" to horticulture that I wasn't willing to try, but this goes too far. I really think that watching professional wrestling is preferable to spending time and money on synthetic plants; at least the actors break into a sweat.

Although I abhor the very idea of this movement, I have to admit that the imitations come close to looking like the genuine article. My father-in-law, for one, was easily fooled by a bogus botanical being. He was once alone, doing repairs on his shore home. When my mother-in-law joined him, she gave him hell when she found water spots on the floor under a fake plant.

Apparently, he had been watering it while she was away.

I suppose we started down this path when radio and TV became so popular. Before then, every child was taught to sing, dance, and play an instrument. In those days, families created their own entertainment. Whether they produced music, wrote letters, or grew gardens, what people had then was a sense of accomplishment. I know Americans aren't writing as much as they did one hundred years ago,* but I always thought horticulture was immune to this type of instant gratification.

It always seemed to me that gardeners enjoyed the process as much as the final results. It's the coaxing of something alive to the heights of horticultural glory that we savor most. And our failures don't cause dejection, because they're really a form of education.

I can remember expressing my disgust one day when I saw fake plants on the stage where a lecture was taking place. My wife, Arlene, didn't understand at first, but I asked her how much she'd like it if a mannequin with a CD of the lecture were wheeled out as a substitute for a live speaker.

Finally, she understood.

For me, it's the very fact that plants are alive that makes gardening so marvelous. They germinate, grow, mature, and sometimes die, and unlike the synthetics, they're not perfect. I think that all of you have experienced certain days when you've gone into a garden that, for that one day, was overwhelming. What made you appreciate it most was

---

*If current-day Americans wrote as much as citizens did one hundred years ago, do you think greeting card companies would have sold $7.5 billion worth of cards in 2001? ("Greeting Cards," Drug Store News, 01917587, 5/20/02, vol. 24, Issue 7, *Business Source Elite*)

knowing that it was changing and that tomorrow it might not look as good. But then, that's life isn't it? And what makes life so exciting is that we don't know what tomorrow will bring.

As for me, I'll continue trying to grow plants in the dark recesses of my house. I may be subjecting myself to endless frustration, but even waking to find every leaf on the floor is preferable to sharing my home with those unchanging, lifeless synthetics.

And perhaps if we get rid of them altogether, my father-in-law won't waste water on them anymore.

An On-Death's-Door Plant Society
-OR-
Annuals on First, Perennials on Second

I have to admit that I'm on the fringes of the garden world and a horticultural pariah. I might as well be living in the sewers of Paris, because while the rest of the world's gardeners do their darnedest to make plants live forever, I remain enamored with annuals.*

I became aware of my lowly place in the horticultural community after I gave a lecture at the Rodale Research Institute. One woman, whom I'll call Patsy, asked me if I had attended the last Hardy Plant Society Symposium. When I told her that I wasn't a member, she looked at me in horror and read me the riot act, saying, *"Then why am I here listening to you?!"*

I found her response surprising, but not shocking.

William Robinson, the early twentieth-century, English landscape designer, railed against the use of bedding (annual) plants. He was unbending in his prejudice and wrote many books (e.g., *The English Flower Garden*) that were read avidly by gardeners on both sides of the Atlantic Ocean. His readers took his words as gospel and Robinson's influence lasts to this day. Perhaps it's an important reason why there's been a slow, but steady, reduction in the use of annuals and the availability of annual seeds.

But having described Robinson's views, it also should be understood that he was writing about large gardens, and I'm in complete agreement with him when it comes to landscaping an estate. However, the average size of today's garden is diminutive by comparison.

---

*The term "annual" typically refers to flowering plants that are started from seed and blossom outdoors during the first growing season. The first freeze in the fall usually kills these plants.

In fact, Gertrude Jekyll, the renowned garden writer and one of Robinson's friends, thought annuals were appropriate for small gardens. I'm sure that if she were alive today and saw my pint-sized backyard, she'd find no fault with my choice of plants.

Don't misunderstand me; I think perennials are wonderful in their place. But you can't escape the fact that the average perennial's bloom time is relatively short. The horticulturists at Pennsylvania's Longwood Gardens know this, so they fill their Flower Garden Walk with 75-80% annuals to produce a gapless riot of color all summer. In my travels, I've seen hundreds of other private and public gardens with flower beds composed of a similar percentage of annuals.

As long as home gardeners understand how an annual "thinks," they can achieve smaller versions of Longwood's Flower Garden Walk. These plants try to produce as many seeds as possible before the first freeze. If they succeed, they'll have plenty of progeny for the next growing season. But the process of forming viable seeds weakens annuals. So, since seeds come from pollinated flowers, the secret to a long bloom season is to remove faded flowers before they form seeds. In response, annuals produce more and more flowers to guarantee that at least some seeds are formed.

Given these facts about a full season of color from annuals, I have to admit my incomprehension. Specifically, why are there thousands of clubs devoted to perennials, but virtually no annual plant societies? There are primrose, rock garden, *Hosta*, delphinium, *Sempervivum*, and *Chrysanthemum* societies, just to name a few. And, of course, there's the Hardy Plant Society, with individual clubs all over the planet.*

The deification of the hardy plant has created a caste system in the botanical world, which is why I wouldn't dream of trying to convince a horticultural organization to let me lecture about common annuals.

---

*Just before this book was published, I performed an Internet search of "Annual Plant Society" using the search engine Google. It yielded only three hits, but they concerned annual meetings of "non-annual" plant societies. A search of "Annual Flower Society" and "Annual Flowering Plant Society" yielded no hits. On the other hand, a search of "Hardy Plant Society" yielded 1,670 hits. I reviewed the first hundred and every one was a web site that focused on perennial plants. A search of "non-hardy plant society" yielded zero hits. The only surprise was that my computer didn't laugh in my face.

And, this state of affairs is such a shame.

When I was a child, my fourth grade teacher, Miss Tolles, introduced my class to the marvels of seed germination. It was my first foray into the world of soil and seedlings, and the process remains magical for me to this day.

Helping a living thing grow from a seed to a plant that quickly produces vegetables or flowers is a miracle that no gardener should miss. In addition to the excitement of seed germination, using annuals gives the flower gardener the chance to start with a clean slate each spring. Empty flowerbeds are like a painter's canvas, allowing gardeners to experiment with color combinations and compositions every year. Artists would scoff at the idea of a certain color always occupying the same space in all their paintings, and I feel the same about flowerbeds.

I admit that each fall I feel wistful when my annuals are killed by the first freeze. But if you grow annuals, you have to accept the fact that although they're gorgeous all summer, they're also like the nobility during the French Revolution — a frosty guillotine awaits each plant at the end of the growing season.

Even so, every other stage — from seed, to plant, to flower production — is worth the extra work in the spring. Any gardener who hasn't experienced "the cosmic secrecy of seed"* is missing a lot of magic. I can't guarantee that each seed will germinate, nor that you won't have heart-breaking failures, but the possibility of failure shouldn't stop gardeners from playing a new horticultural hand.

Having declared my love for annuals, you'll understand why I think a worldwide annual plant organization, with thousands of local chapters, should be formed. I'd be in favor of calling it The On-Death's-Door Plant Society. The name may focus on the most depressing part of the growing season, but it would be catchy enough to attract attention and garner new members. In addition, it would finally allow me to come to closure on this issue.

What I anticipate is a reprise of my conversation with Patsy — the gardener who wears "perennial blinders," and for whom the word "annual" will always be an adjective and never a noun.

---

*Marjorie Kinnan Rawlings, *Cross Creek*, (New York: Time Life, 1966) 380.

When she asks me, once again, if I've attended the latest Hardy Plant Society Symposium, I'll say, "No, Patsy, there was a meeting of The On-Death's-Door Plant Society on the same day."

"What on earth is that?" she'll ask.

"It's a garden club that celebrates plants that always die before they're a year old."

Patsy will look at me narrowly and say, "You're pulling my leg, right?"

"Absolutely not. We've got plenty of members and have 'annual' meetings once a month."

"I'm confused. How can you have annual meetings once a month?"

"Well, Patsy, everyone agreed it would be nuts to have an 'annual' meeting once a year."

"So, let me get this straight. You meet once a month because you can't wait a year for an annual meeting, but it's still an annual meeting?"

"Now you've got it, Patsy!"

"*I don't know what the hell I've got!* You all love plants that die, and your annual meetings are once a month?"

"Absolutely."

"I think you're all insane. Why would gardeners grow plants that can't even live for a year?"

"So we can have glorious, colorful gardens all summer."

"But don't some of these plants die in the summer?"

"No, we know they won't."

"Art, how could you know that?"

"Anyone who attends our monthly 'annual' meetings could answer that."

"I've never been so confused about gardening in my life."

"Let me help you out, Patsy. I'll send you a book about on-death's-door plants. After you read it, you can come to one of our 'annual' monthly meetings so you can take our test."

"A test? You have a test at your monthly meetings?"

"Sure do."

"What kind of test?"

"Oh, Patsy. I thought you'd have figured that out. Each month, new members stand in front of everyone and we give them an 'annual' check-up."

"Huh! You what?!"

"Well, so long, Patsy. I hope I'll be seeing a lot more of you real soon."

"German small town homes with ever-present compost heaps."

Bernard Wolk (1945)

Front Yard Dictators

Love your neighbor, but don't pull down your hedge.
- Benjamin Franklin

Do you have family members who were involved in World War II? If you do, you've probably seen their dog-eared, faded photographs from when they risked their lives so that we could live in freedom.

My father was a pharmacist in a MASH unit that followed the front lines, from North Africa to Europe. Over my lifetime, I've seen the countless photos he took, showing the good times and the bad — from happy days in Sicily to the horrors of the Dachau death camp. Nothing shocked me more than those ghastly concentration camp pictures, but then another photo caught my eye. It was less shocking, but seemed otherworldly to a U.S. gardener. The photograph showed German town houses with five-foot-tall compost piles in *front* yards.

Of course, my reaction was because of my peculiar vantage point as a U.S. citizen. After all, when was the last time you saw a compost pile in an American front yard?

It seems that we can paint our houses any color we like and can plant anything in our backyards, but the front yard is the yardstick of community conformity. If you don't agree, try plowing under your lawn and replacing it with 'Silver Queen' corn. I guarantee that you'll be shunned within two weeks and, when the local police chief says to "round up the usual suspects," your name will be at the top of the list.

Surely, it wasn't always this way in America. Neither Native Americans, nor conquistadors, nor Pilgrims went around judging their neighbors based on what plant species were next to the entrances of their homes.

It wasn't until the mid-nineteenth century that garden designers espoused the idea of front yard conformity. In 1870, famed landscape architect Frank P. Scott argued that the front yard should become a vital link in the creation of a community park. He "sought the collaboration of town and city dwellers in leaving their front gardens as an uninterrupted sweep of green lawns, with individual private gardens being kept to the back of the property. It was an expression of American egalitarianism, for Scott felt that hedges and fences ... were an indication of 'how unchristian and unneighborly we can be.'"*

By 1927, the idea of making your front yard part of a public park became nothing less than a show of patriotism. Frank Waugh, Professor of Agriculture at the University of Massachusetts, noted, "Everyone who is patriotic and wants to do something for his country will promote ... the development of ideal American homes. In the Old Country the primary planting is a hedge along the street front. The American Home is open to the street. The plants, instead of forming a hedge, are pushed back against the foundations of the house...."†

What Scott and Waugh were saying was that a community park composed of uninterrupted front yards should take the place of personalized front yards. Perhaps this explains why so many of our communities did not set aside true public green spaces in town centers, as is commonly seen in Britain.

I can remember talking with one English gardener who found our unfenced front yards very confusing. She said that fenced front yards were very common in her country and asked, "How do you know where your garden ends and your neighbor's garden begins?"

Of course, the opposite view is held in the United States, where most homeowners view front yard fences as something akin to the Cold War's Berlin Wall. It's this mindset that's given me second thoughts about erecting a fence. What surprises me is that, considering past events, I still care what my neighbors might think about such a fence. In the front yards of my various homes, I've had flowers trampled upon by street athletes as well as plucked by kleptobotanical villains. Even worse, I've had entire plants that I started from seed dug up and stolen in broad daylight. I've also had dictatorial neighbors tell me exactly what groundcover I should grow in my front yard (meaning only grass)

---

*Howard Loxton, *History of the Garden: Its Evolution and Design* (New York: Barnes and Noble Books, 1996), 92.
† Loxton, 92.

and how I should prune my shrubs (meaning always in the shape of a box, meatball, or Roman column). Incredibly, even neighbors who've seen my plants damaged or stolen, look at me as if I'm an extraterrestrial whenever I tell them I'm considering a front yard fence to protect my plants.

For something as subjective as front yard dictatorship, I can't provide statistically significant data on its prevalence, but I can certainly share a few anecdotes that run from the innocuous to the illegal.

My first story is about a woman I dearly love: my Aunt Gert. In all the years I've known her, I don't think I've seen a bit of dust in her house or an unkempt blade of grass in her front yard.

She lives in a row home in Philadelphia, Pennsylvania, which means that she and her neighbors share a common swath of grass. My Aunt Gert has the eye of a soaring eagle and can detect the smallest bit of her neighbors' crabgrass barely poking out of the ground. She views it with the same alarm that a public health doctor might view an air duct containing Legionnaire's bacteria. In other words, she thinks that a blade of crabgrass is like an epidemic that's about to infect her lawn.

Her eagle eye isn't limited to crabgrass. It can also detect the movements of her neighbors. When they leave the house, Aunt Gert swoops into action. She dashes to the offending weed, eradicates it, and bolts back to her side of the lawn.

It's quite possible that her neighbors don't even notice the crabgrass. It's also possible that they hate crabgrass as much as my Aunt Gert, but find it unnecessary to unearth it themselves. At this point, I wonder who's fooling whom.

My next story is anything but innocuous:

Friends of ours bought a large, new, expensive home. After moving in, they went to a nursery and bought evergreens in two-gallon containers to plant in the front and along the side of their home.

The day after they were planted, they found a note in their mailbox from their next-door neighbors that read, "You're in an expensive development, so to help maintain the value of nearby houses, you should plant more mature trees and shrubs. You can purchase them at the following nurseries ..."

And, my friends had foolishly thought that *they* owned their front yard.

My last anecdote concerns Jill, whose favorite tree is in her front yard. Unfortunately, she has a neighbor who hates the tree because it blocks his view. He's already asked Jill to trim or remove the tree, but naturally she's refused. When she first turned down her neighbor, she thought the issue was settled. Then, about a month later, a tree surgeon knocked on her door.

"Hello, I'm removing that tree over there," he said, pointing to the tree in question. "So, as long as I'm here, do you have any other tree work you'd like me to do?"

As Jill discovered, her neighbor had unilaterally decided to alter her landscape — a trait common to many front yard dictators. It was only by coincidence that she was home and that the hired tree surgeon was entrepreneurial enough to knock on her door, otherwise the tree would have been turned into mulch.

I've heard so many stories like Jill's, that I'm convinced the only long-term solution for front yard gardeners is to erect a fence. We'd certainly get our share of scorn because of the front yard rules set forth five generations ago. But now that we've started a new millennium, I think it's time for a different front yard paradigm to emerge — one that allows gardeners a full range of creative expression. So, let's not look to our front yards to create quasi-parks. Instead, let's support the creation of true public green spaces in our communities.

As for the front yard dictators who think I'm being unpatriotic if I put up a fence to protect my plants, I have this to say: I've had to put up with your TV cable coursing through my front yard and your children's feet crushing my flowers. So perhaps it's time for you to accept something a bit different in the front of my house, whether it's a wooden fence, a vegetable garden, or even a compost pile.

11

GARDENERS TO LOVE

A Senior Citizen Limbos Through Life

WHEN I ATTENDED MY FIRST South Jersey Organic Gardening Club meeting, an elderly gentleman was showing slides of his yearly horticultural activities. Everything went smoothly until he started to fumble while looking for a switch on the projector. Someone in the audience called out, "Put on those glasses of yours, Taylor!" Whereupon, the speaker donned one of his famous gadgets: a pair of glasses with little glowing spotlights attached to the side of each lens. He found the sought-after switch, and the program proceeded amid the raucous laughter of the club members.

It marked the beginning of my acquaintance with Len Taylor, a man more full of life, fun, and the joy of gardening than anyone you or I will ever meet.

In an age of compromised values and confused ideals, Len lives by one simple motto: "Feed the soil and the soil will feed you." He's a man ninety-years-young who has the stamina of someone half that age; a man who used his own hands to build the house he's lived in for more than sixty years; and a man who's a vegetarian, growing virtually all the food he eats.

Most importantly, he's been feeding the soil of his Pennsylvania garden with organic matter for all of those sixty years. Like most people he puts his leftover garbage down a disposal. But unlike you or me, his garbage disposal is in the garden, so the effluent can be caught and mixed with his soil.

After many decades of surface composting,* his soil is black, fertile, and has the elasticity of a 24" sponge. His lifelong love affair with the soil has yielded vegetables that are simply astonishing.

---

*In surface composting, raw materials are spread on the soil where they either rot in place or are mixed into the underlying soil.

All organic gardeners have heard the mantra a thousand times: Vegetables grown organically look and taste better than those grown non-organically. Although there may not be scientific proof about the better taste of organic produce, Len Taylor's vegetables prove what unbelievable results can be accomplished by gardening organically: sixteen-foot-tall tomato plants, five-foot-tall leeks, and twelve-foot-tall pea vines. His plants dwarf the competition, literally.

What this means is not just huge plants, but huge yields. He has enough vegetables to feed himself for the year, with plenty left over for his family, which adds up to seven sons and daughters, twenty-seven grandchildren, and three great-grandchildren.

Len is a Renaissance man not so much trapped, as reveling in the twenty-first century. A short history of his life to date reveals his curiosity, intelligence, ingenuity, and resourcefulness; attributes that all great gardeners share.

Born in 1912, he spent the first eight years of his life in Philadelphia. Back in the 1920s, everyone in his neighborhood gardened, and Len loved it from the start. He learned how to grow plants organically from his parents, who used the manure from their chickens, ducks, and guinea hens for fertilizer.

After Len finished eighth grade, his father declared high school wouldn't be worth it for him, since he was "a little too stupid anyway!" It didn't take long for Len to prove him wrong.

He started working at a gas station and immediately showed exceptional mechanical capabilities. By the age of sixteen, he bought his first used motorcycle. It began one of the great loves of his life, and, to this day, it remains his preferred mode of transportation. He recently received a trophy from a motorcycle club for being the oldest active biker.

In 1937, he went to Philadelphia Electric Company to take a test for linemen applicants; but when he arrived, he was told a mistake had been made and that he couldn't take the test, because only high school graduates could apply.

An angered Taylor bristled at the wasted time, and insisted that they at least let him take the test, high school diploma or not. They relented and he eventually got the top score of the thirty-six applicants. It created such a stir that the president of the company insisted on meeting this self-educated marvel. Needless to say, he was hired and eventually became a supervisor, the highest position available to non-college graduates. Len supplemented his income for thirty years by photographing weddings on Saturdays, and he eliminated the middle-man by developing the photos in his self-built darkroom.

In 1938 Len and his wife Trudy built his current home, a Cape Cod, using their own hands and blue prints bought for 25¢ from a mag-azine. The studs in the walls came from thrown-away cross-arms from Philadelphia Electric Company utility poles. The entire home cost them only $2,000 to build.

Over the years he acquired extra lots for a few hundred dollars, so that he could have the extensive vegetable garden of his dreams. In the 1940s he used more cross-arms to build his greenhouse — a structure he still uses to start his seedlings.

Taylor began gardening at his new home, but with poor results. He didn't have to look far for a cause: his soil was lousy.

So began a lifetime of feeding the soil. When an older couple hired Taylor to wire their home, his charge for the job was only the manure from their cows. He also composted his neighbors' leaves to produce what he calls "black gold."

More recently, his gardening chores have become easier. Since his town added a composing facility, he no longer has to scour the neigh-borhood for discarded leaves. Instead, Len built a trailer to haul the material back to his home. In an average year, he uses about five hun-dred wheelbarrows of leaf mold in his 8,000-square-foot garden.

The surface of his topsoil is approximately two feet higher than it was back in 1938. After sixty years of loving care, his soil is a soft, black, crumbly mass that begs roots to enter it.

How soft is it? Not long ago, this nonagenarian fell off a 16' lad-der while harvesting fruits from his two-story tomato plants. He hit the soft-as-a-mattress ground, suffered no ill effects, and went right back up the ladder.

Taylor starts all his plants from seed, using his own starter mix of 80% leaf mold, approximately 20% sphagnum peat moss, and varying amounts of lime and raw kelp.

By late summer his tomato plants reach the top of his 15' cages. He especially loves it when cars screech to a halt and the passengers gawk at his giant plants. Len invites strangers to tour his vegetable garden and entertains them with stories about his horticultural exploits.

Aside from the perfect soil, the most conspicuous features in Len's garden are the many inventions used to spur his plants to greater horticultural glory.

His prized water collection system can store up to five hundred gallons. He collects every drop from the roof of his home into huge, interconnected barrels. After only ½" of rain, every barrel is filled. Using a sump pump and a hose, he uses this water for his vegetable plants. Len never uses a single drop of tap water, which he believes would be detrimental.

Taylor uses raised, insulated beds to grow lettuce and carrots all winter. The beds have clear plastic over them, supported by loops of PVC pipe. There are thermostatically-controlled 100-watt bulbs under the plastic, two per bed, which are set to come on when the temperature drops below 40°F. By February his raised beds are crammed with mature vegetables ready for harvest.

Besides a strict diet that includes vegetables, fruits, and chickweed, Taylor says you can live longer by "appreciating every single day, each sunrise and sunset, and taking 'worriment' away from yourself." He suggests that you shouldn't share woes with your family at mealtimes; instead, everyone should tell a joke.

There's a big part of Len Taylor that makes you want to get as close as you can to him, to have his magic rub off onto you. He laughs at the transitory nature of life and jokes about subjects that others would consider macabre. Len delights in telling anyone about a cemetery owner who called him when he turned eighty. The man wanted to sell Len a plot in his perfectly manicured, weed-free, final resting place. Len turned him down flat, telling the owner that he "didn't want herbicides and pesticides seeping into [his] bones!"

But with all the upbeat humor, good food, and inventions helping him live a long life, it's difficult for me to forget that one of his gadgets almost caused his death several years ago.

Len used to drive his car into his garage, then hit a switch on the dashboard to activate the automatic garage door he installed. As the door started coming down, Len would run out as fast as he could to avoid the descending door. It was his very original version of the limbo.

One day, he neglected to turn off his car when he started his Olympic dash for the gold. While he and his wife dined upstairs, deadly carbon monoxide seeped into their house.

It would have killed them both if not for the television quiz show, *Jeopardy*.

Luckily, his friend Pat watched it with him every evening. On that particular night, he knocked at Len's door, but no one answered. Pat heard the TV on inside, so he was suspicious. When he entered the house, he found Len and his wife flat on the floor. An emergency squad was summoned, and eventually the pair was sent by helicopter to a Philadelphia hospital.

They both pulled out of it — barely.

The next day, there was Taylor on TV talking jauntily to a reporter about his adventure, as if it was just one more day in the life of this inventor/gardener.

A week later, at a garden club meeting, someone showed a videotape of Len's TV interview; so again he was the center of attention. He basically laughed the whole thing off and didn't let his near-death experience affect him; except perhaps that he uses his motorcycle more and his car less.

So from now on, whenever I think about what life will be like for me when I reach my eighties, I'll think of Len Taylor: A man who always lives one day at a time, who's an eternal optimist, and who hasn't lost the sparkle in his eyes that was probably there over eighty years ago.

Cruising in South Jersey

I'VE TRAVELED TO SO MANY GARDENS throughout the United States, and although many of them were glorious, my fondest memories are derived from the people I've met in each of them. One such person is a friend who lives near my home in New Jersey, and her story shocked me more than any I'd heard before or since.

She's a sweet lady named Pearl Wade, whose lovable nature seems to attract everyone like a magnet.

Pearl learned about growing plants as a young child, when she worked barefooted on her family's farm. She doesn't live there anymore, but still owns the land and spends afternoons and weekends at the farm tending her vegetables. Although there were too many weeds to make her vegetable patch a candidate for a *Better Homes and Gardens* article, the plants were yielding just as much produce as a perfectly manicured garden. I soon realized that "perfect" vegetable patches might not be worth the long hours of compulsive tending.

Besides, her weeds aren't worth mentioning compared to another threat: rattlesnakes live in a nearby stream and occasionally visit local farms and backyards. So although area residents have deeds for their properties, none of them ever argue with rattlers about easement rights. Pearl's story about her husband, Ed, once protecting a neighbor from a rattlesnake was enough to make my blood curdle.

Wade's life is composed of one fascinating story after another. By an unlikely coincidence, her husband and brother were at opposite ends of the globe during the most famous events involving the United States during World War II. Ed was at Hawaii's Hickam Field in 1941 when Pearl Harbor was attacked, and her brother, Lawrence, was in the worst of the fighting during D-Day in Normandy.

In 1945, Ed was ready to move on with his life. He married Pearl and they bought a home about three miles from her family's farmhouse.

By fits and starts, they developed Wade's Salvage into a profitable business.

Unfortunately, Pearl's brother was never the same after the war. As his health failed, she cared for him in the old, family farmhouse. On the day Lawrence died, Pearl left everything in the house the same, including the teacup and saucer that her brother used that morning. It remains exactly the same today, uninhabited. Her story was a case of life imitating art — her enshrined farmhouse evoked memories of Miss Havisham from Charles Dickens's *Great Expectations*, who, after being jilted at the altar, kept her home exactly the same for decades after her ill-fated wedding day.

In 1996, Pearl told me about a neighbor's beautiful front yard, which had scads of native pink lady slipper orchids in bloom every May. Her vivid description had me salivating, so we made a date to see the orchids when they were at their peak.

On the appointed day, I drove to Pearl and Ed's business, but none of her descriptions of their salvage yard prepared me for what I saw: It was a metal menagerie, where it seemed that everything made of iron or steel could be found, and towering overhead was the tallest non-tropical bamboo I'd ever seen. To complete the scene, they had a plane fuselage in their front yard!

Otherworldly would be too bland a description of the setting; other-galactic would be more appropriate.

When Pearl came out, we drove about a mile to her neighbor's home. On the way, she constantly twisted her body left and right, making me think that she had a medical condition. When I asked if she was OK, she laughed and said that she was, "always on the lookout for more salvage being thrown away. Art, you never know what treasures people will get rid of. Maybe I'll see something we can take back to the salvage yard."

I was more than a little relieved that she didn't see another plane fuselage along a curb.

At her neighbor's front yard, there was an extravaganza of pink lady slipper orchids — dozens and dozens. I'm not an orchid expert, but I'd be surprised if there's anywhere else on earth where pink lady slippers could be found in such abundance. Incredibly, the non-gardening homeowners had thought the orchids were weeds and were going to pull them out. Fortunately, someone told them about the treasure they possessed, so the plants were saved.

That evening, my wife, Arlene, was more interested in my description of the salvage yard than the orchids. We're both movie lovers, so without any hesitation, I told her that it was exactly like the eerie junkyard in the popular rock-and-roll film *Eddie and the Cruisers*, which starred Tom Berenger and Ellen Barkin. She listened, wide-eyed in amazement.

The next day I talked with a policeman who came into the library I managed, and told him about my experience of the previous day. When I mentioned Wade's Salvage, he said, "Oh yeah, the place where *Eddie and the Cruisers* was filmed."

I was thunderstruck.

"Are you sure you're talking about the rock-and-roll movie from the 1980s?" I asked.

"Definitely; it created a stir in the area because the filming took months."

I stood as still as a marble column. I never had a photographic memory when it came to college textbooks, but I was beginning to realize that I had an excellent cinematic memory. It had been more than thirteen years since I had seen *Eddie and the Cruisers*, but the brief scenes of the junkyard were vividly tucked away in my brain.

That day I rented a videocassette of the movie and looked very closely at the credits, but there wasn't one word about Wade's Salvage. I was baffled.

At the next garden club meeting, I spoke to Pearl and plied her for details about the movie. Sure enough, they had done some of the filming at her salvage yard.

She told me that one day a nervous man drove to her home, knocked on her door, and said he wanted to use Wade's Salvage as a setting for a movie called *Eddie and the Cruisers*. Pearl mentally jumped two steps ahead and thought, "Wow, this guy really did his homework. He actually knows the name of my husband!"

Weeks passed and Pearl forgot about the nervous man and the movie. Then one day, a limousine pulled up to their curb and out stepped studio executives with contract in hand. Ed and Pearl signed it and soon thereafter the preparations for the movie began.

The filming reduced their business to a trickle, but Pearl loved every second. She made friends with everyone and even had a campfire party for the stagehands. Pearl especially enjoyed a guard who ran into her house late one night after hearing strange noises. The sounds turned out to be a mooing cow and a hooting owl. She laughed and calmed the guard's nerves by educating him about life in the country.

In spite of the disruption, her neighbors loved the filming. Although the production company had a firm rule that only Ed and Pearl's family should have access to the set, somehow their nearby "family" swelled to more than one hundred people because all their neighbors claimed to be relations.

When the movie was released, Pearl took a hidden lunch to a local theater and ate it while watching the film. Her critique was to the point. She thought the film was "real nice."

I enjoyed her stories, but remained baffled about the lack of a film credit. "Why," I asked "didn't they give Wade's Salvage a credit at the end of the movie?"

Pearl said, "Well Art, we had the choice of either having a movie credit or $5,000. Now how much business do you think a salvage yard would generate from a credit in *Eddie and the Cruisers*? So we took the cash.

"But that's not the end of the story. That $5,000 became $20,000 when they asked for permission to do filming from inside our house and on our roof. It was toward the end of their stay, so we knew we could get more than another $5,000. We asked for $15,000 and got it. The funny thing is, they never did a bit of filming from our house or roof. So, we got an extra $15,000 and they got nothing."

Like I've implied before, just when you think it's the garden that's going to astound you, it ends up being the gardener.*

---

*If you watch *Eddie and the Cruisers* very closely, you'll notice a sign that reads "Wade's Salvage," just before the actors drive into the salvage yard. So Ed and Pearl's business got a bit of advertising after all.

Sylvia – I Love You,
Let Me Count the Ways

I'm still married.

I still love my wife.

But she's got company, namely Sylvia Lin.

So let me explain.

Sylvia is a top Philadelphia Flower Show exhibitor who's as competitive as the rest of us, but there are important differences. For many exhibitors, blue ribbons are not just awards for their superior plants; they're an addictive dose of personal superiority. People look up to you, give you attention that you've never had before, and want to be your friend. They think that if you've won a blue ribbon at the Philadelphia Flower Show, you're an expert horticulturist who knows how to identify and care for every plant on the planet.

But like the best athletes, Sylvia lives "in the present" and is addicted to the excitement alone. She's one of those strong, quiet people we occasionally meet, whose self-confidence comes from within, lasts a lifetime, and doesn't need material success to be maintained. This is immediately obvious when you talk to her after she's won a blue ribbon. I've never heard her say, "I won a blue ribbon for my *Begonia*." What I always hear her say is, "My *Begonia* won a blue ribbon." There's a tremendous difference between the two statements.

After hundreds of blue ribbons and numerous Horticultural Sweepstakes Trophies, I don't think a single award ever made her feel superior to anyone.* On the other hand, she definitely feels that way

---

*When I interviewed Sylvia for this book, she could neither recall when she won her first Horticultural Sweepstakes Award, nor how many times she'd won it. This had nothing to do with a bad memory. Sylvia is very intelligent and has an excellent memory. The point is that once the thrill of winning an award is over, there's no reason for her to recall it. Her inner strength makes it unnecessary for her to flout her past achievements. For Sylvia, new thrills lie ahead; old ones disappear like a vapor.

about her plants. There's really no difference between this and nurturing parents who imbue inner confidence in their children.

Given this trait, it comes as no surprise that she was a nurse. Under her watchful eye, her patients undoubtedly reached their summit of health. By extrapolation, this must have been true of her human children and is definitely true of her botanical children: every plant bespeaks her love, talent, and attention. They simply glow.

Her bond with her plants is life-long, and no one steps between her and them. She doesn't even let her husband water her plants, and the fact that he's a neurosurgeon doesn't make a bit of difference.

Nothing would have thrust Sylvia into the horticultural limelight except for one thing: When she was a teenager, her sister took her to the Philadelphia Flower Show, where she was captivated. Twenty-five years later, she competed in the show for the first time and won an honorable mention ribbon for a fern. When she saw the award next to her plant an incredible thrill coursed through her. She was so excited that she had nurses find her husband at work so she could share the moment with him.

It took two more years of trailing flower show judges for her to learn what kind of plants win blue ribbons. Once she finished this Pinkerton-type of flower show education, her horticultural skills were ready to shimmer.

The third year, she won her first blue ribbon. And although her first honorable mention ribbon gave her an electric thrill, this was more like a lightning bolt.

For the successful exhibitor, this type of excitement would be difficult to handle even if it were spread over fifty-two weeks; but when it's concentrated into one week, it overwhelms you, even if you're competitive by nature.

Perhaps that's why Sylvia Lin's personality changes somewhat during the Philadelphia Flower Show. For fifty-one weeks of the year, Sylvia acts dignified and angelic. But during the week of the Flower Show, she may act angelic at times, but it's a good idea to stay out of her way. During that one week she has a laser-beam focus in her pursuit of the blue nylon and silver cups.

I started entering plants in the Show in 1979, just a bit before Sylvia. By 1982, I hadn't met Sylvia, but her plants were becoming irksome. I'd enter a great plant in a category and she'd enter a perfect plant. Can you guess who won the blue ribbon and who got the red one? After a few years, I started hating the color red.

I didn't meet Sylvia until 1994. It had taken a dozen years, but Sylvia was starting to notice my name — especially the very few times my plants won blue ribbons in classes she entered.

Despite competing against one another, I soon felt genuine affection for her, and these three stories will help you understand why.

****

Falling in Love — Part I

In 1996, I was trying to win a second Grand Sweepstakes Award at the Philadelphia Flower Show, and Sylvia and Mrs. Dorrance Hamilton were vying for the Horticultural Sweepstakes Award. During that week, the public relations staff at the Pennsylvania Horticultural Society thought the three of us should be interviewed on The Home and Garden TV Network.

By then I had already done two gardening segments for the Discovery Channel, so I said yes right away. Mrs. Hamilton also agreed, but Sylvia didn't like the idea at all. Even so, I thought I could convince her to say yes.

I told her that very few people would be watching the recording session. I also mentioned that during the taping of a television program, many "takes" are recorded, and that the best sections are pieced together, so mistakes are eliminated.

She remained unconvinced.

Then I looked her in the eye and said, "Sylvia, I'll have my arm around you the whole time to give you physical and emotional support."

That was exactly what she wanted to hear, so she agreed.

On the appointed morning, we went to a designated area of the show and got our instructions from the hostess, Barbara Damrosch,* and the director.

---

*Aside from hosting garden TV shows, Damrosch is a successful book author and lecturer.

The videotaping went smoothly except for one moment. Damrosch asked me a question, and in my usual extroverted, gesticulating manner, I explained how gardeners compete at the Philadelphia Flower Show. When I finished talking, I put my arms down, but forgot to put one around Sylvia. That's when she reached over for my arm and, quite deliberately, put it around her.

It was at that moment that I felt love for her. I had so much admiration for her horticultural capabilities, but during the interview she wanted to have the security of a friend she could trust. I was that friend and forevermore, I felt honored.

****

Falling in Love — Part II

As I've mentioned before, Philadelphia Flower Show exhibiting is exhausting — not unlike the mountain stages of bicycling's Tour de France. Only the competitor with the most heart, stamina, and talent arrives at the finish line first.

Although I'm younger than Sylvia, she has twice my energy. In 1997, after a week of exhibiting, the last day of judging had arrived. Most of us had a deep, inner exhaustion, but not Sylvia.

I was sitting in a chair against a wall, too exhausted to get up and see what ribbons I had won. On the other hand, Sylvia was crackling with energy. She was looking at her hanging plants to see what awards they had earned. But unfortunately, plants were the only things she had her eyes on. While she walked rapidly from one competitive class to another, I marveled at her endurance — at least until she became a human bowling ball.

Four elderly women were standing between Sylvia and the results she sought. With her eyes "plantward," she bowled into the ladies and sent them helter-skelter. Luckily, no one fell or was injured, but Sylvia came out of her reverie and made sure her human bowling pins were OK.

I laughed hysterically.

It was so funny because Lin carries herself with great dignity, so this disaster was completely out of character for her. That day, I thanked Sylvia for giving me such a comedic experience. She smiled, and with plenty of irony in her voice said, "Why thank you so much for noticing, Art!"

****

Falling in Love — Part III

At one flower show, I was looking over some rare succulents that were for sale. It just so happened that Sylvia was at the same place, at the same time. As I studied the plants, my eyes came to rest on an attractive one (*Orostachys spinosus*) that had perfectly balanced, whorled segments.

Sylvia saw me examining the plant and edged a bit closer. I looked at the price and decided it wasn't too high. Sylvia came even closer and sidled-up next to me as I got out my wallet.

"You don't want that ugly thing," she said.

"But Sylvia, look at the whorled symmetrical segments — it's gorgeous."

"You'll never be able to grow it in your greenhouse," she countered.

"Sylvia, what are you talking about? I have cacti that do just fine in my greenhouse, right alongside my potted bulbs."

Then it hit me: The competitive side of Sylvia was showing.

I said, "Hold on! Did you just buy one of these and don't want me to compete with you?"

"Stick to bulbs, Art!" she responded, and began walking away.

I laughed so hard I was doubled over, but then realized that she was paying me a compliment. Sylvia was one of the top succulent growers in the United States and thought my horticultural skills were good enough to challenge her supremacy.

That sealed my platonic love for Sylvia.

Some years I only see her during Flower Show week, some years several times. But I feel fortunate to call her a friend.

There's one last "grace note" I should add to these stories: One day, I gave a lecture to Sylvia's garden club and related my three "love stories." The audience laughed, but later I wondered if I'd embarrassed her.

A few days later, I got my answer. It was a note from Sylvia that asked the question, "Does your wife know that we are in love?"

12

BARELY FICTIONAL STORIES

A Visit to Hortiholics Anonymous

I OPENED THE DOOR TO THE MEETING room, walked in, and sat in the last row, trying not to be noticed. The bright ceiling lights had a warm, welcoming glow — as warm as the convivial atmosphere among the almost one hundred people in attendance. I had arrived none too soon; the group's leader was advancing to the podium to begin the proceedings. He had a gentle smile and looked out on the audience without seeming to stare at anyone.

"Welcome everyone, and I do mean everyone, new members, old members, as well as guests. My name is Bill, and I hope you all had a good week. Would anyone like to start us off?"

After a brief pause, a woman slowly stood up and took a few seconds to begin talking. Looking down at the ground, in halting, stammered words, she forced herself to say, "My name is Mary and I haven't bought a plant in six months."

Applause and murmurs of approval rose from the audience. Apparently, this was the first time Mary had talked to the group about her problem.

"You see, before I became a gardener, I had a checking account that was never overdrawn and credit card bills that I always paid on time."

The members nodded, saying, "We know, Mary. We understand."

"But then ten years ago, I was on a winter trip to New England and my husband stopped the car at Logee's Greenhouses in Danielson, Connecticut."

Many in the audience shook their heads, as if they had been to Logee's and knew exactly what Mary was going to say next.

"I had never been inside a greenhouse before, and the only plants in our apartment were a philodendron and an African violet that my husband took care of. I really didn't want to stop. I had no interest in gardening, but my husband said, 'Just ten minutes, Mary. Just ten minutes.'

"I protested, but decided I might as well have a look inside. So I got out of the car, trudged through the snow, and went in. I guess I don't have to tell any of you how intoxicating it was, with the orchids, ponderosa lemon tree, begonias, and other tropical plants. I was enraptured by the smells and sights that surrounded me.

"Once inside, I seemed to have no concept of time. My husband came over with a small potted begonia and apologized for taking so long. Thirty minutes had passed, but I felt as if I had just entered the store.

"Then I noticed the shock on my husband's face. He looked at my shopping basket and saw that I had already collected two dozen plants. He asked, 'Who are those plants for?' and was doubly shocked when I told him they were for me. Before we left, I had seventy plants and a bill of $300.

"Of course, that was only the beginning. I started buying light fixtures, fertilizers, grow lamps, germination mats, and more plants, lots more plants. My hobby became an obsession, and before I realized it, houseplants literally started to crowd out my marriage. Plants were everywhere: in the kitchen, the bathroom, and even in the closets, where I had fluorescent lights installed. Soon, I started sacrificing vacations, because I couldn't trust anyone to take care of my plants.

"The final straw was when I started lying to my husband about our finances. I had spent so much on my hobby that debt overwhelmed us. That's when Mike left me. He had been enabling me for so long, that he knew leaving was the best thing for both of us."

Tears streamed down Mary's face; then the man in the next seat got up and put an arm around her.

"I finally realized I had to do something. That was six months ago, and it was when I came to my first Hortiholics meeting. It was only the first step, but an important one. You've all been so wonderfully supportive, especially Bill. There were so many lonely nights, when I was ready to open a garden catalog and order more plants. Bill was the one who stayed on the phone and talked me through one crisis after another.

"It's taken six months, but last week I threw out all my plants, and that's when Mike came back to me."

Mary turned and looked into the tearful eyes of the man next to her.

"This is Mike, everybody. He came back home yesterday."

Applause filled the meeting room, and I noticed that more than a few people were shedding tears of their own.

"I guess that's about it, except that I want to thank every one of you and say that I can finally face tomorrow with hope. But I'll take it just one day at a time, just one day at a time."

There was more clapping as well as smiles of understanding. Almost everyone in the audience was acquainted with the same kind of daily battles that Mary had fought.

Although I felt emotionally drained after Mary's story, the meeting wasn't even half over.

Next, there was a young woman who had received $2,000 from her parents for a down-payment on a car, but instead spent it on a horticultural trip to Italy and Greece.

Then a man got up and told us that he had been stealing plants from nurseries for decades. He had endured many encounters with the law, but they did nothing to change his addiction. It was only after attending years of Hortiholic meetings that his craving for plants was controlled.

Of all the tales that were told that night, I especially remember the woman who had a fetish for blue ribbons. She had gone from one flower show to another with the goal of winning enough blue ribbons to cover every wall in her house. It had been two years since she had competed in a flower show, but she said she still had problems. The Philadelphia Flower Show was approaching and she knew it would take all her willpower to ignore the hype in the media.

On and on it went, one saga after another, with the same applause and words of encouragement from the audience after each person's story.

But not everyone joined in.

I noticed one man who never nodded with the others, never applauded, and never offered words of encouragement. When the proceedings ended and everyone was enjoying snacks, I went over to him.

I introduced myself and slowly, reluctantly, he looked up. He said his name was Barry and that he'd been coming to these meetings for two years. He had heard all the heartrending stories and tried all the Hortiholics Anonymous techniques, but they didn't help. He made a good living as a computer consultant, but spent every penny on plants, seeds, garden equipment, and horticultural trips.

Barry seemed hopelessly depressed.

At last! This was the reason I had come. I had endured all the blubbering and sanctimonious talk about treatments for hortiholism long enough.

I went over to Barry, put my arm around him and said, "Look, you have nothing to be ashamed of. In fact, I know a group where you would be respected, even admired. We would welcome someone with your problem. We all have your problem; we just accept it.

"We have great meetings, trips, speakers, and an excellent newsletter."

Barry looked me in the eye and I could tell I had him. The hook was set and it was time to reel him in.

"Here's an application to become a member of the Horticultural Society of South Jersey. Just fill it out and send your check to our treasurer."

Barry cautiously took the application, stuck it in his pocket, and winked at me. Then he whispered in my ear, "See you at the next meeting."

I walked out of the room and smiled. The night had been a triumph.

Are You Zoned Out?

We've all known or read about alcoholics who went through their entire lives bouncing from one binge to another. They'd lose their jobs, families, and fortunes, but would say they were only "social drinkers." In today's parlance, they were all "in denial," meaning they couldn't admit that they had a problem.

Of course, virtually every person with an addiction has, at some point, gone through denial. Although alcoholics are the most readily recognizable group that denies the obvious, other examples abound. Perhaps the most famous was identified by Elisabeth Kubler-Ross, who described the five stages of behavior in people with a terminal disease. The first stage is denial, then anger, bargaining, depression, and finally, acceptance.

If you enjoy movies, watch *All That Jazz*, a semi-biographical work about choreographer Bob Fosse. It clearly and chillingly shows the five Kubler-Ross stages in a man dying of heart disease.

While dealing with terminal illness is the most extreme example of the Kubler-Ross stages, I think there are plenty of other areas of human behavior that involve the same five stages. I can recall many other gardeners and myself going through these stages when selecting garden plants.

Here's the typical scenario:

It's 4°F outside in mid-winter and a garden catalog arrives in your mailbox. Professional photographers supply the photos for these catalogs specifically to make winter-weary gardeners salivate and grab their credit cards.

And, they succeed.

The only problem is that some of the most alluring plants in the catalog are native to a climate warmer than yours.

The U.S. Department of Agriculture has helped gardeners by

defining plant hardiness areas, known as zones, in North America.* In an average winter, Zone 1 has temperatures below -50°F. As zone numbers get higher, the typical lowest winter temperature is warmer, with Zone 11 having temperatures above 40°F all winter.

Using zonal information can help gardeners choose plants that will survive local winter weather. But unfortunately, this information fails to make a dent in our consciousness. Because of our desire to broaden the spectrum of plants in our gardens, we buy specimens that aren't hardy in our zone. Perhaps somewhere within our craniums we tell ourselves that we'll provide some protection in the winter: a little burlap here, a little extra mulch there.

By doing this, we deny the fact that this has never made any difference in sustaining tender plants through the wicked winters of the Northern United States. If this sounds at all familiar, you're suffering from what's known as "zonal denial."

So come winter, you tuck these plants under a pile of oak leaves, behind some yew bushes, or against the south-facing wall of your house. Then you go into the warm confines of your home for the next four months.

The north wind blows, and the mercury dips so low that you wonder if it will ever come out of the glass bulb at the bottom of your outdoor thermometer. You warm yourself by the fireplace while your abandoned Hawaiian transplants are outside doing anything but the hula.

On the first warm Saturday in the spring, you rake the leaves next to the house and discover the blackened remains of your tender plants. Normally this would be depressing, but it's been a year since you bought them, so by now you're ready to prepare a spot for new mail-order plants.

After a few more years of this behavior, the bank account gets lower, the flowerbeds turn blacker, and the compost pile gets larger. Finally, after you've killed thirty mail-order plants, you're ready to admit that you have zonal denial.

---

*A plant's hardiness relates to its ability to endure a specific range of low temperatures. My area of Southern New Jersey is designated Zone 6b, meaning that plants must be able to withstand temperatures as low as -5°F to survive our winters. A copy of the USDA Plant Hardiness Zone Map can be found on the Internet at http://www.usna.usda.gov/Hardzone/ushzmap.html.

But just like the pattern described by Kubler-Ross, getting past the denial stage only leads to the second of five stages.

Next comes "zonal anger" — boiling, seething, red-hot anger. How dare the elements destroy your plans for a sub-tropical paradise in New Jersey, Indiana, or North Dakota. Your anger knows no bounds and you take it out on everything and everyone around you. That's when your spouse has the good sense to tell you to shape up or ship your botanical backside out!

So you do whatever it takes to relieve your anger, whether it's counting to one hundred, taking deep breaths, going to a movie, mowing down bowling pins, or smashing a few dozen golf balls.

The next day, you wake up refreshed and head outside to get the day's mail. And there it is — a summer garden catalog. You're past zonal denial and zonal anger, and are ready for a bit of "zonal bargaining." You swear to Mother Nature that you'll pile the mulch higher and add more burlap if she'll watch over your plants during the winter. You aren't hit by lightning on the spot, so you assume Mother Nature has accepted your deal.

You fulfill your end of the bargain, but Mother Nature sends along the worst winter since *Tyrannosaurus rex* was roaming in Wyoming. The temperature plummets to -10°F and water pipes are freezing everywhere. Snow doesn't disappear from the landscape until April 1st, and you're recovering from the worst case of cabin fever since most Americans really lived in cabins.

You step outside and make the mistake of looking for the sub-tropical *Camellia* you tucked in the earth last June. Of course, all that's left are a few sticks fit for next year's kindling. Eventually, it occurs to you that bargaining with Mother Nature is about as effective as bargaining with a loan shark packing a Magnum.

You realize there's nothing you can do short of changing jobs, saying farewell to your friends, uprooting your entire family, and moving south. You give this serious thought for a few hours and mention this scheme to your spouse, who gives you a look that translates into, "Do you want to live to see your next birthday?"

So, the next step begins, and slowly, insidiously, a dark, black, invasive "zonal depression" sets in. And when the next plant catalog comes, it plunges you even deeper down the well of botanical despair.

All the classic signs emerge: You start to give away shovels, pots, bulbs, and perennials; and on sunny days, you don't even venture from the house.

But just when you've given up hope of ever pulling out of your depression, your spouse takes desperate action. Up until then, your significant other would never have suggested that the family visit a large, public garden. After all, you always made it such torture for everyone by spending the entire day obsessing over each plant. But to rouse you from your stupor, your spouse drags you to the car and drives to what was previously your favorite place on earth.

In the conservatories, you recognize many of the zonal denial plants that you ordered from catalogs. And, finally an epiphany seeps into your neurons: If professional horticulturists have to keep these plants in a conservatory, what hope do you have of keeping them alive out-doors during the winter?

At long last you've reached "zonal acceptance," and your gardening life can continue. When fall arrives, you can peruse a garden catalog and appreciate the beauty of sub-tropical plants without being tempted to order them. Your addiction to these plants is over, and you decide to buy native plants to adorn your garden.

Since you've rededicated yourself to beautifying the backyard, your family takes the risky step of giving you a gift certificate to a mail-order plant business. So, you glance through the company's catalog and discover an orange tree that they claim is hardy in the Northern United States.

Is it possible? Well, what's the harm?

You submit an order for three of these citrus plants, but a moment of terror sweeps over you because you're afraid the old pattern may be reasserting itself. Fortunately though, you realize that it's not you who thinks citrus trees can be grown outdoors in your zone, but the mail-order company. Your mistake is simply that you believe it.

Of course, believing in the viability of plants as stated in many plant catalogs is a different behavior disorder altogether — it's called gullibility. And any of us who think we aren't gullible from time to time is practicing yet another denial. Still, I wouldn't get too concerned. Our personal defects are just like the gardens we create: we have to be content to take on one challenge at a time.

Remember? *Gone with the Wind* author Margaret Mitchell ended her book with the words, "Tomorrow is another day."

She must have been a gardener.

Plant 9 from Outer Space

There it was, outside my car window. I slowly steered to the side of the dusty road in Georgia and gradually came to a halt. I looked to my left and saw it again — whatever it was. My eyes were riveted, for I had never seen anything so huge and monstrous, at least not anywhere outside of a movie theater showing a 1950s science fiction film.

During my childhood, films about creatures attacking a metropolis were produced continuously. At the time, I had the discrimination of a housefly, so I plopped down quarter after quarter every Saturday to see them. Watching such films now makes me wonder if a body snatcher borrowed my brain until I went to college.

They were real clunkers.

I think they could safely be put into any one of three categories: (1) bad scary movies, (2) really bad scary movies, and (3) movies that were so bad, they were scary.

A list of some of the worst would include:

- *Them* — about ants that grow to the size of mastodons because of nuclear testing in the U.S. desert.
- *The Deadly Mantis* — about a huge, life-threatening praying mantis that's freed from a melting glacier.
- *Tarantula* — about a scientist who invents a nutrient that's too nutritious, making animals grow too fast and too large. Can you guess which arachnid escapes from his lab to cause havoc?
- *It Came from Beneath the Sea* — in which a skyscraper-sized octopus develops a distaste for the sea and a taste for humans.

As bad as those films were, they don't come close to the so-bad-it-hurts film by Ed Wood: *Plan 9 from Outer Space*. Bela Lugosi (best known for his starring role in *Dracula* in 1931) was cast as the "Ghoul

Man," but died when filming was just getting started. Instead, Wood substituted a chiropractor who "saved" the film because he had a hairline similar to Lugosi's. The substitute paraded around with a cape over his face, so only his hair showed. There were also cardboard tombstones, a female vampire, paper plate flying saucers, as well as three zombies that aliens raised from the dead to take over the earth — a theme common to science fiction films of the era.

In my college years, I learned that the menacing creatures in these films were really metaphors for the threat of world communism. As a child, I attended an elementary school that held atomic bomb drills, and I lived in a home with a garage that was a designated civil defense shelter. It made me the perfect audience for these films: they were aimed straight at my subconscious fears of the red, meaning communist, menace.

My memories of movies about huge animals and *Plan 9 from Outer Space* were hidden in my subconscious and would have stayed there, but for my visit to the Southeastern United States.

When I stopped on the Georgia highway, I saw thousands of trees draped by miles of green, leafy sheets. After a few minutes, I realized that the vine was kudzu — also known as the "Plant That Ate the South." Here, in real life, was a botanical giant preying upon any tree in its path. It was like the 1950s science fiction films I had seen, except it wasn't a member of the animal kingdom that had become monstrous, but a plant. Looking closer, it was impossible to discern a single tree leaf, because the vine was draped like sheets across the top and sides of every tree. Kudzu had started its onslaught by sending its sinuous fingers up the sides of a tree, at first caressing, but finally strangling its prey.

It was nothing less than botanical genocide.

A bit further down the highway there was a house that appeared to have been shuttered and locked for two years. A green tidal wave of kudzu had splashed against the house and was beginning to submerge it in a sea of chlorophyll. I could only imagine its owner, transferred to Europe for a work assignment, then returning in another year to find not a home but a house drowned by kudzu.

I was witnessing a life form that was taking over the earth. *Plant 9 from Outer Space* would be an obvious name for a film about this creature — only the film wouldn't be science fiction, but a documentary; and the menace would be green, not red.

When I got home, I did some research and learned that kudzu isn't native to the United States. It turns out that the Japanese brought it to the 1876 Centennial Exposition in Philadelphia. The fact that it was tenacious and grew fast was noted by the U.S. Soil Conservation Service, which eventually recommended that it be used to control soil erosion in the 1930s.

So, they planted it on purpose.

Since that ominous day, it's blitzed its way throughout the Southeast. To date, kudzu has covered approximately 8 million acres; and, each year, another 120,000 acres comes under its domination.

Eight million acres is a lot of land — equivalent to 21,500 square miles. To put it in perspective, consider that it is the approximate area of the countries of Jamaica and Belize combined. If those 8 million acres were composed of trees instead of kudzu, there would be enough lumber to build millions of homes or print hundreds of millions of books. If it were farmland, it would yield enough food to feed 32 million people for a year. And if the land were left undeveloped, think how marvelous it would be to have another 8 million acres of parkland.

My southern encounter changed my view of weeds forever. To this day, whenever my neighbors complain about weeds, I laugh and ask them if dandelions ever ingested their house.

But speaking of dandelions, did you know that they're native to Asia and Europe? This begs the question of how this scourge of suburbia made its way to this country in the first place. A best guess is that its seeds were either on the clothes of Europeans or the hides of their animals that came to the New World. All it took was one springtime nap in a meadow and the alien seed was planted. The dandelion was off and flying in every wisp of wind, never to be controlled.

Other alien weeds have slipped through our borders and have given gardeners fits for hundreds of years. A partial list includes crabgrass, thistle, chickweed, curly dock, wild garlic, ground ivy, henbit, prickly lettuce, pigweed, purslane, and sorrel. In other words, almost all the weeds you've come to know and hate.

In spite of all the land captured by kudzu and all the back-breaking hours of labor caused by the other weeds I've mentioned, they're nothing compared to the problems caused by the really villainous members of the botanical world: poisonous plants.

There's a virtual cornucopia of them that have crossed our borders and installed themselves in our woods and meadows. These include poison hemlock, Jimsonweed, various nightshades, and stinging nettle, just to name a few. These plants have been responsible for skin rashes at best and death at worst. One can only wonder at the ease with which these botanical scourges of North America have invaded our nation.

Our border guards may check soil and plants for diseases and insects, but how many times do they check your clothes and shoes for seeds that are hitching a ride? The answer, of course, is almost never.

We quarantine produce and animals that may be infected with dangerous microbes, but I've never heard of a single case of noxious seeds found on skin or clothing being confiscated.

But just because eradication of the above-mentioned alien plants would be all but impossible, we shouldn't give up the fight against new botanical scourges. I do, in fact, have a course of action to suggest:

1. When people want to cross the border into the United States, their clothes and shoes would be confiscated by the government and shredded, sterilized, and recycled into new garments.
2. Like the decontamination procedure used in the science fiction movie *Andromeda Strain*, humans and other animals crossing the border would enter a chamber where their outer epidermal layer would be zapped off.
3. Government botanists would check seeds imported from foreign countries. Any seed not recognizable would be planted and grown in government labs and, if necessary, a DNA analysis would be used for identification. Any non-native weed seeds would be destroyed, and the responsible company wouldn't be permitted to export seeds to the United States for at least two years.
4. Anyone knowingly transporting noxious plants or their seeds into the United States would face criminal prosecution and possible deportation.

These tactics may sound a trifle extreme, but the next weed crossing our border may have twice the gallop of kudzu, three times the potency of deadly nightshade, and snares one thousand times the size of Venus flytraps.

After seeing kudzu in action, I couldn't help but remember that paleontologists have estimated that 99% of the species that have ever existed on earth eventually became extinct. So, while you're watching a PBS special about the possibility of human extinction caused by global warming, I suggest that you also keep a wary eye on seemingly innocuous plants that could be engulfing your house when you're not looking.

And if you think I'm exaggerating, take a trip to rural Georgia next summer and have a peek at kudzu in action.

Just don't get too close. I don't want to open a newspaper one morning and read that the nickname for kudzu has been changed from "The Plant That Ate the South" to "The Plant That Ate the Gardener."*

Kudzu-draped trees, Central Georgia

---

*Admittedly, this section isn't a fictional story as implied by the title of this chapter. Only my suggestions cross over to the fictional realm … but just barely.

The High Cost of a Salad

Helen hated golf.

She didn't hate playing golf, although she tried to play once, and only once. No, the thing that Helen hated was what golf was doing to her husband, her marriage, and their budget. To her, golf wasn't a sport anymore; it was a formidable enemy, an enemy that was winning.

As she drove home from work, she said aloud, "Why did Harry have to pick golf as a hobby?"

Upon arriving home, she grabbed the day's mail and headed inside. Once seated at the kitchen table, she slowly began to open each envelope.

Minutes later, Harry parked his car and slowly scuffled up the front steps. He slouched as he carried a briefcase that appeared to weigh fifty pounds, though it was only one-tenth that weight.

"Hi, honey," he yelled from the living room as he closed the front door.

Helen was distracted by the mail, so it took a few seconds before she said, "Hello, dear" in a monotone voice.

Harry headed straight to his easy chair, sat down, and pushed a button that sent the chair into a reclining position. He let his body sag into the cushions and didn't move for a full minute. There were dark circles under his eyes from the lack of sleep and hard work he had endured that week. When he felt less exhausted, he lifted his newspaper and began reading the sports section.

Helen threw junk mail into the trash, read a letter from her sister, then noticed an envelope from MasterCard. With a sense of dread, she opened it, and when she saw the amount that was due, ten years of repressed anger and frustration exploded. She had had enough and headed straight for the living room.

"Harry, what the hell do you think you're doing?!"

Startled, Harry threw his newspaper into the air, then said meekly, "Just sitting here trying to read the paper."

"*Don't get smart with me, you know what I mean!*"

"No, I don't. What are you talking about?"

Harry avoided Helen's gaze and tried to sink down into his easy chair.

"*Our charge card statement just came, that's what I'm talking about.*

"Look, I know you work hard all week and need a hobby, but the cost of your playing golf every weekend is ridiculous. Last week you spent $250 to play at that new course in Pennsylvania, and that's nothing compared to the $10,000 it cost to join the country club. Then there's the $3,500 for your new clubs and the golf trips you take every winter. Where will it all end?

"I'll tell you Harry, I just don't get it. Every time you come home from playing golf, you're so angry and frustrated that it takes you a week to recover. Then you're out the next weekend spending big bucks to get angry all over again.

"I think it's time you considered another hobby — one that's less expensive."

"But Helen, I've been a golfer all my life. I don't know if I could get interested in another ..."

"Wait a minute, Harry, I've got an idea. Why not try gardening? You might even save us a bit of money by raising salad vegetables."

Harry's mind raced, trying to search for some defense against his wife's tirade. Then he remembered his friend Art and figured out the right course of action.

"Y'know Helen, maybe you're right. Perhaps I will give gardening a try next year. That's a great idea!"

Satisfied with her victory, Helen backed away and headed into the kitchen. She couldn't see the widening grin on Harry's face that was hidden behind his newspaper.

Several months later, as Harry shoveled the snow from his front walk, he heard a truck approaching. He looked up and saw Betty, the mail carrier, park next to him. He greeted her as she handed him that day's mail. Harry put down his shovel and began to look through the envelopes. Eventually, he found what he'd been expecting for several days. Harry smiled and put the mail into their mailbox.

An hour later, Harry sat on his easy chair awaiting the inevitable. Finally, Helen came into the living room and stared out the front window.

"I think the mail's arrived, Harry. I'll go get it."

Helen walked outside, grabbed the mail, and returned. As she went to the kitchen, Harry peered over a magazine, watching her.

Helen sorted the mail and noticed an envelope from MasterCard. She opened the bill and saw the total that was due. Her face reddened and her eyes opened so large that the pupils seemed to get lost in the surrounding white.

After using her calculator, Helen scurried straight into the living room.

"Harry, take a look at this statement."

Her husband took the four sheets of paper, coolly perused them, and handed them back to Helen.

"Well, what's going on, Harry?"

"It looks about right to me," he said calmly.

"Looks about right! Are you crazy?

"Jones and Eagle, $3,272; Granley Seeds, $253; Jimco Greenhouses, $25,047; Electrified Fences, Incorporated, $5,027; Bellinger's, $2,953; Danley's Mulch, $2,841; Jarvis Electrical Services, $1,477; Ace Plumbing, $2,231; and Ernie's Engines, $5,210."

Helen shot the numbers out like bullets from a machine gun, each one making Harry flinch.

"Well? I want an explanation."

Harry had carefully plotted his course of action, so he had a planned response.

"Well, Helen, you suggested that I take up gardening, so I figured I might as well do it right. I gave Art Wolk a call. You know him; he's the guy who exhibits at flower shows and was president of the local garden club. Who'd be better than Art to teach me how to get started in gardening?"

"Yeah, yeah, I know about Art Wolk. He's the loony gardener who was in the newspaper before the Philadelphia Flower Show."

"That's right, Helen. Well, anyway, who would be better than Art to get me started? So, he told me what I needed to become a real gardener: First, he said I had to have a greenhouse to raise great flower and vegetable plants. So that explains the electrician, plumbing, and Jimco bills.

"Next, there are the flats, soil mixes, pH meter, germination mats, shovels, trowels, rakes, pruning sheers, knives, sprayers, and cold frames from Bellinger's.

"Then, I needed soil, mulch, fertilizer, shrubs, and trees from Danley's, and the seeds from Granley. Plus, I had to have a rototiller and tractor from Ernie, so that explains that bill."

"And, the electric fence! What the hell is that for? Are you starting a state prison?"

"No, Helen. Art said there's a high population of deer around here that would love to dine on all the vegetables plants you want me to grow. So we have to get an electric fence to keep them away."

"And, the Jones and Eagle bill?" Helen said.

"Well, Art thought I should get Wellie boots from them, so while I was at it, I decided I might as well also get a proper gardening wardrobe, too."

"So, let me get this straight. Are you telling me that just because I suggested that you take up a hobby that might provide a salad, it ends up costing us over $48,000?"

"Well, actually Art said that's just for starters. He's really got me excited about exhibiting in the Philadelphia Flower Show next year, especially in the bulb classes. That should run us about $2,500 in bulbs and another $1,500 to wire several cold frames with heating cables. Then there's the truck I'd have to rent, and the ..."

"YOU CAN STOP RIGHT THERE!

"I don't remember seeing any of this stuff around here. Have any of these things been delivered yet?"

"Well, no," said Bill, "I told them not to send anything until March because ..."

"Never mind!" Helen replied.

She turned on her heels and left the living room. In the kitchen, she grabbed the phone and began calling each of the companies listed on the charge card statement.

"Hello, Jimco, this is Helen Duffman. I'm calling to cancel an order for a greenhouse. Yes, that's right, the $25,047 one my husband ordered."

When Helen finished canceling all the garden-related purchases, she made one more call to their local travel agent. Finally, she slammed down the phone and went back into the living room.

"Well, Harry, you can forget about gardening. Our household budget wouldn't survive another three months with you as a gardener. So, I've done the only thing that could save our bank account as well as our marriage: I've booked you on a two-week golf trip this summer in Scotland.

"Thank goodness there's still one inexpensive hobby left."

"Helen, you're absolutely right! I may not be able to raise a salad by playing golf, but at least it won't ruin our marriage."

Harry's admission softened Helen's heart. She leaned over, gave Harry a kiss, and left the room.

When she was out of sight, Harry discretely pulled out some stationery and began writing to his friend.

"Dear Art — How can I ever thank you enough ..."

"...and this is specimen #487 found while in
Fiji...I know, I know...thrilling isn't it..."

13

ON BECOMING A GREAT, BUT NOT TOO SERIOUS, GARDENER

Why Serious Gardeners Shouldn't Act Serious

WHEN YOU ATTEND A TYPICAL GARDENING program, there are serious lecturers with serious pictures of serious plants, planted by serious gardeners that are shown to an audience with too many people who take gardening too seriously. Admittedly, it helps gardeners if a lecturer dispenses information that will broaden their botanical horizons, but what some lecturers haven't realized yet, is that this only happens if the audience stays awake.

Most garden lectures include, or are limited to, projected images shown on a screen. For an image to be discernable on a screen, the lights must be turned off. And, when the lights are turned off, it sends a signal to the average human, and that signal is to start sawing wood ... as in snoring ... very loudly.

I happen to find that a snoring audience helps neither my reputation nor my confidence. So, I've come up with a solution: Garden lectures should be entertaining first and informative second. For the average person who's listened to other types of programs, this isn't a new concept. You know which lecturers have kept your attention, and invariably they relied on something called a sense of humor.

This is absolutely essential, because keeping the audiences' attention is a battle that should never be taken lightly. In fact, I've been told that the average audience is divided into three groups: those thinking about sex, those thinking about things they need to get done, and those who are paying attention. Consequently, the first job of a lecturer is to keep the third group alert, while snapping the other two groups out of their reveries. Obviously, any lecturer who can hold the attention of all three groups is sensational. To do this, lecturers can't simply be dispensers of information or they'll lose everyone's attention. Good lecturers know they have to add humor and that it has to be added consistently throughout the lecture.

The problem with gardening programs is that many lecturers have decided that they can give effective lectures that could all be titled: "Let's Look At These Pretty Pictures Together." Lecturers who give these types of programs must have unshakable confidence, because within ten minutes they not only lose those with attention-deficit disorder, but also members of Mensa.

When I first started to use humor in my garden lectures, an interesting thing happened: many laughed along with me, but some people in the audience didn't know what to make of it. In short, they were shocked, and had looks on their faces that could be translated as, "He wasn't trying to be funny at a gardening lecture, was he?" I had a strong feeling that they thought a gardening program was something akin to a memorial service and that laughter was in bad taste.

Since then, I've given about 150 lectures over the years, and have to admit that no matter how much humor I try to throw at my audience, there are still those whose approach to gardening is as serious as President Kennedy when he took us to DEFCON 3 during the Cuban Missile Crisis. So, to help those of you who have a problem lightening-up and laughing at gardening in particular and life in general, I offer some advice.

I have to admit that I'm not trying to make the world a better place by dispensing these aphorisms, but that I'm being self-serving. I don't want any competition while I lecture, and snoring has a way of becoming more infectious than the common cold. It's forty laughs that I'm after, not forty winks.

****

1. Accept the notion that by gardening you're not going to figure out a unified theory of the universe and win a Nobel Prize. Leave that kind of serious work to theoretical physicists. It also might help you to know that physicists not only have active minds, but even a sense of humor.

2. Realize that you're absolutely unessential in the big botanical world. Plants were here long before we showed up and they somehow managed to survive without 5-10-5 or manure tea.

3. Following from number two, you should understand that humans who try too hard to keep plants alive are usually doing more harm than good.

4. There's no perfect place for plants, so when you move the same perennials from one side of your yard to the other, then back again, then forth again, your neighbors have probably turned off their TV and are enjoying the comedy show you're providing.

5. We make mistakes, plants die, and it isn't a big deal. Don't start the "woulda, coulda, shoulda" game. You can't bring back yesterday, or as my Uncle Jerry would say, "December 6, 1941 was a beautiful day in Pearl Harbor."

6. The next time you do something really stupid in your garden, just laugh. People who have lost the ability to laugh at themselves need to give themselves a break. If you think there's a gardener on earth who doesn't make the same kind of stupid mistakes, you've been hoodwinked.

7. Make friends, work, and garden with people who can laugh at themselves. Eventually, the ones who can't will poison your life.

8. Understand right now, that you only get so many days above ground. Do you want to spend them pushing people away by acting deadly serious about gardening, or do you want to spend them being a lively, avid gardener who laughs whenever you get the chance and is surrounded by friends?

9. Pursue what makes you curious. It will take your mind on a lifelong journey. It will also keep your synapses firing, make you fun to be around, and fascinating to others, regardless of your age. If there's a fountain of youth, it's curiosity.

10. Only you know what makes you happy, and no one else can tell you what that is. You'd be amazed at the number of people who are stuck in an unhappy existence their whole lives doing what others expect of them. Think about what makes you happy and do it. In the words of famed mythologist Joseph Campbell, "Follow your bliss."

11. Don't wait until you retire to do the things or go to the places you've dreamed about. By that time, you may be too infirm or perhaps you won't even live that long.

12. If you do live long enough to retire, don't retire when you retire. The people who are happiest and live the longest seem to be the ones who always have some new exciting career awaiting them. Plan your next career as carefully as you plan all the other facets of your retirement. During my next career, I'll be a full-time horticulturist. What have you chosen?

The Thrill of Occasional Failure,
The Agony of Constant Success

A schoolchild plants a flower seed in a cup of soil and waits. A day passes, two days, a week, two weeks, three weeks. His classmates all have seedlings to show off at home, the child nothing. Dejected, the child feels a sense of failure, but in the end is left with a question: Why did this happen?

The child that failed, grew into a man who was able to answer the question, while his classmates who succeeded could not. He became a gardener; they didn't.

The lesson, of course, is that failure can be an opportunity, not a defeat.

Since becoming a garden lecturer, I've been trying to pass along the lesson of my non-germinating seed. But invariably, there are people in the audience who ask me, "How can I be guaranteed to have success?" I answer the question as best I can, but feel bad for them. They're missing the real excitement in gardening: the worry, the caring, the love, the hope, the occasional devastation, and the days of sheer bliss that can only come after experiencing some failure.

Bobby Jones, Teddy Roosevelt, Malcolm X, and Richard Nixon may not have been gardeners, but they each have a lesson for us. They all experienced magnificent success as well as abject failure, and knew that it wasn't possible to have one without the other.

Here's what they each had to say about the importance of failure:

Bobby Jones, who, in 1930, became the first golfer ever to win all four major golf tournaments in the same year, said, "I never learned anything from a match I won."

Jones had become part of the national consciousness in 1916, when, at the age of fourteen, he made it to the quarterfinals of the U.S. Amateur. Surely, everyone thought, this wunderkind would start winning major championships in short order. But it was not to be.

It was another seven years before he won his first. There were seven lean years during which he had to learn to handle his temper as well as his golf ball. But from each failure there was a lesson to be learned, and as the lessons mounted, he finally became a champion — one of the best ever.

President Teddy Roosevelt, in his "Man In The Arena" speech, talked eloquently about the importance of participation, even if it means failure.

He said, "It is not the critic who counts.... The credit belongs to the man who is actually in the arena, ... who strives valiantly; who errs, and comes short again and again; because there is not effort without error and shortcoming; ... who at the best knows in the end the triumphs of high achievement and who at the worst, if he fails, at least fails while daring greatly, so that his place shall never be with those cold and timid souls who know neither victory nor defeat."

Malcolm X was a convicted felon who overcame his early failures to become one of the legendary civil rights leaders of the twentieth century. He noted that there are two kinds of failure: the failure that can happen when you try to succeed and don't, and the more tragic failure that occurs when you don't even try.

He said, "Children have a lesson adults should learn, to not be ashamed of failing, but to get up and try again. Most of us adults are so afraid, so cautious, so 'safe,' and therefore so shrinking and rigid and afraid, that it is why so many humans fail."*

Richard Nixon certainly knew about stupendous success and failure. In fourteen years he went from vice president, to failed presidential and gubernatorial candidate, to a president who enjoyed some unqualified successes, but who became the only president to resign.

On the day he left the White House he was able to summon himself to say, "It is only a beginning, always. The young must know it; the old must know it. It must always sustain us, because the greatness comes not when things go always good for you, but the greatness comes and you are really tested, when you take some knocks, some disappointments, when sadness comes, because only if you have been

---

*Malcolm X, *The Autobiography of Malcolm X*, reissue edition (New York: Ballantine Books, 1992), 448.

in the deepest valley can you ever know how magnificent it is to be on the highest mountain."

So from four very divergent men, we have a lesson in life that can be used in gardening. I'm not saying that you should embrace failure, but that you should embrace the possibility of either failure or success. Doing this can be exhilarating, because you're never so alive as when the outcome is unknown.

You might as well face it: Failures are important. And when it comes to gardening, failures aren't to be feared, but to be used for the opportunity they provide for gaining expertise.

In the world of horticulture, it's easy to compare yourself and your garden to expert gardeners and their world-class plants and gardens. But you should realize that for every blue-ribbon-winning plant they exhibit, there are probably just as many disappointing plants left at home. And for every glorious garden you visit, there probably have been many years of experimentation and ignominious failure. Always remember that great gardeners leave trails of the dead and dying plants that helped them stretch their horticultural wings.

Ray Rogers, an exhibitor who raised the standard of excellence for everyone at the Philadelphia Flower Show, talks just as freely about his failures as his successes. I can remember walking through the show with him one year when he told me which categories he doesn't enter because he always "kills those plants." The important thing to note is that at least he tried many times and didn't "play it safe."

There are so many other endeavors in life in which we play it safe: We take jobs with more security than career possibilities. We go on vacations to places that we've been to a dozen times. And we go to the same restaurants and order the same food.

In each case, we're doing something to play it safe and avoid the possibility of disappointment or failure. But there's no reason to play it safe when it comes to gardening, since gardening isn't about playing it safe. It's about a racing heart, dazzled eyes, and incredible surprises. It's questions brought, answers sought, failures fought, and successes wrought. But most of all, it's about embracing life and all its possibilities.

So, when you look through garden catalogs, let your eyes wander to pages that hold new possibilities and adventures. Throw yourself into an endeavor that will force you to learn a new skill. Grow a type of plant you've never grown before. And be sure to sow seeds that may grow into something magnificent or perhaps not grow at all.

With all my heart, I wish you enough success for you to continue gardening and enough failure to make you into the great gardener you're destined to become.

Afterword

Books are the children of every author, and like children, some are planned and some are not. When I began writing this book, I had no idea it would become one. No one expected it of me, nor did I expect it of myself. This book began when I began my life, for I've put many of my experiences into it.

Some people can plot a course for their life to follow, step-by-step. I freely admit that I've rarely had the capability to do so. The experiences you read about in this book mainly happened through sheer luck. I had a teacher who brought seeds to class one day. I couldn't have planned that. There was an Italian family who lived in an apartment above us. They planted a garden that astounded me. I couldn't have planned that either. I was fortunate to live in a neighborhood with a gardener who planted bulbs next to the same path I walked upon every day. And my wife brought home a potted coleus that fascinated me as I watched it grow. I didn't plan that, she did.

I was born in Philadelphia, Pennsylvania, which was a blessing. If one draws a circle around Philadelphia that has a radius of eighty-five miles, it will probably encompass more garden clubs and horticultural organizations than anywhere else on earth. In addition, there's an indoor flower show in Philadelphia each March that rivals the magic of Houdini. That flower show became and still is a very big part of my life. Without it, I doubt that you'd be reading these words.

My capability to grow bulbs for that flower show was noticed by horticultural organizations that hired me to give bulb-forcing workshops. A press release for one of my programs found its way to a television producer, which ultimately led to two tapings of me teaching a Miss America to grow bulbs.

How does one plan such events?

Through exhibiting and succeeding at the Philadelphia Flower Show, I had stories to tell. By telling my first story, I became a published author. Again, this was more serendipity than planning. To continue having magazine articles published, I had to provide pictures. To supply photographs, I took photography workshops. One class was taught by a garden editor from *Better Homes and Gardens* with whom

I eventually worked to produce two articles, one of which contained my picture.

I combined my career as a librarian with my capability as a gardener, and started a garden for children. It just so happened that the ground next to the library was of the right size and location to create a garden. The story of that garden flowed more from my heart than my brain. That story was published in a magazine and won an international writing award. How could I ever have planned this?

I joined a garden club and was eventually asked to be the president. When I became president, the editor of the newsletter asked me to write a monthly column. I said yes, but wanted it to be different. I wanted to write about gardeners, not garden plants. Eventually, those writings made me decide to write a book about people not plants. Again, if I had never been president of the Horticultural Society of South Jersey, you wouldn't be reading these words. At no time did I ever seek to be president, I was simply fortunate enough to be asked.

If I had made a steadfast plan for my life at a young age, very few of these events would have happened. Instead, life planned me.

One makes of life what one can. You can make goals, but the world can spin them into orbit. If everything you plan for your life really happens exactly as you wish, when you wish, is it a better life? Or, is it better to leave a large percentage of your life open to whatever may happen? Which life is more exciting? Which is the greater adventure?

Whatever happens to me during the rest of my life, I choose for it to be an adventure. I just hope that one plan doesn't swerve. I plan to be a gardener and to be around gardeners all my life.

I can't be sure what may happen tomorrow, but that's exactly what I want.

Dear Reader,

I hope you've enjoyed reading *Garden Lunacy: A Growing Concern*. As you now know, the stories in this book weren't limited to my gardening experiences. I freely admit that I might never have written *Garden Lunacy* unless other gardeners — and non-gardeners — had shared their hysterical gardening adventures with me.

Before this book was published, I began giving *Garden Lunacy* lectures to garden clubs and other organizations. Following each program, I was delighted that fellow-gardeners came forward to tell me their own tales of garden lunacy.

I'm certain that many of their stories ultimately will be used in the sequel to this book. So, I'd like to invite you to share your stories as well. And, if any are used in the next version of *Garden Lunacy*, you'll receive a free, signed copy.

You can send your stories to me by mail (AAB Publishing Editorial Dept.; P.O. 749; Voorhees, NJ 08043), through my web site (www.gardenlunacy.com), or e-mail (aabpublishing@aol.com).

Happy Gardening!

Art

GIVE THE GIFT OF *Garden Lunacy: A Growing Concern* TO YOUR FRIENDS, FAMILY, AND COLLEAGUES

Check your local bookstore, order here, or visit
www.gardenlunacy.com

☐ **YES**, I want _____ copies of *Garden Lunacy: A Growing Concern* for $26.95 each.

☐ **YES**, I am interested in having Art Wolk speak or give a seminar to my company, association, school, or organization. Please send me information.

Include $3.95 shipping and handling for one book, and $1.95 for each additional book. New Jersey residents must include applicable sales tax. Canadian orders must include payment in US funds, with 7% GST added.

Payment must accompany orders. Allow three weeks for delivery.

My check or money order for $_____ is enclosed.

Name _____

Organization _____

Address _____

City/State/Zip_____

Phone _____ E-mail _____

Call (856)-751-8286

Make your check payable (and send) to:

AAB Book Publishing LLC
P.O. Box 749
Voorhees, NJ 08043

Books may also be purchased at www.gardenlunacy.com.

COLOPHON

Composition by AAB Book Publishing LLC, Voorhees, NJ
(www.aabpublishing.com) performed in QuarkXPress
The jacket text is Cochin; jacket display type is Greco Adornado.
The text type is 11.5 on 14.5 Times New Roman x 27 picas.
Printing and binding by Thomson-Shore Printing Company
The text paper is 60 lbs. Thor White (recycled)
Cover material: Arrestox B

This book was printed on recycled paper.
85% total recovered fiber / 30% post consumer